REA

DO NOT REMOVE
CARDS FROM POCKET

THE
JUKEBOX

---

and Other

Essays on

Storytelling

Farrar

Straus

Giroux

_____

New York

THE

JUKEBOX

———

and Other

Essays on

Storytelling

———

PETER HANDKE

Translated by

Ralph Manheim and

Krishna Winston

LIBRARY OF CONGRESS CATALOGING-IN-PUBLICATION DATA
Handke, Peter.
[Essays. English. Selections]
The jukebox and other essays on storytelling / by Peter Handke ;
translated by Ralph Manheim and Krishna Winston. — 1st ed.
p.   cm.
Published separately in German under the titles Versuch über die Müdig-
keit, Versuch über die Jukebox, and Versuch über den geglückten Tag.
I. Title.
PT2668.A5A249   1994   834′.914—dc20   94-4790 CIP

CONTENTS

Essay on Tiredness 3

Essay on the Jukebox 47

Essay on the Successful Day 121

ESSAY

ON

TIREDNESS

———

Translated by

Ralph Manheim

In the past I knew tiredness only as something to be feared.

When in the past?

In my childhood, in my so-called student days, in the years of my first loves, then more than ever. Once during midnight Mass, sitting with his family in the densely crowded, dazzlingly bright village church, the child breathed in the smell of wax and woolen cloth and was overcome by a tiredness that struck with the force of a sickness.

What kind of sickness?

The kind that is said to be "nasty" or "insidious"—for this was a nasty, insidious tiredness. It denatured the world around me, transforming my fellow churchgoers into felt-and-loden dolls that were hemming me in, transforming the resplendently decorated altar in the hazy distance into a torture chamber enhanced by the confused rituals and formulas of the servers, and the sick, tired child himself into a grotesque elephant-headed figure, as heavy and dry-eyed and thick-skinned as that animal. My

---

tiredness removed me from the substance of the world, in the event the winter world of snowy air and solitary sled rides under the stars at night, after the other children had gradually disappeared into their houses, far beyond the fringes of the village, alone, winged with enthusiasm: utterly present, in the stillness, in the whirring of the air, in the blueness of the ice that was forming on the road —"it tingles" is what we used to say of that pleasant cold. But there in the church the child, held fast by tiredness as in the grip of an Iron Maiden, experienced a very different kind of cold, so much so that in the very midst of the Mass he begged to go home, which just then meant no more than "out." Once again I had spoiled one of my parents' rare opportunities, becoming rarer as the old customs died out, for social contact with the neighbors.

Why must you always accuse yourself?

Because even in those days my tiredness was associated with a feeling of guilt, which intensified it and made it acutely painful. Once again I had failed my family: one more steel band tightened around my temples, a little more blood drained from my heart. Decades later, a feeling of shame comes back to me at the thought of that tiredness; but strangely enough, though my parents later reproached me with one thing and another, they never mentioned my attacks of tiredness.

Was the tiredness of your student days similar?

_____

. . .

No. The guilt feelings were gone. In lecture halls, on the contrary, my tiredness made me angry and rebellious. Ordinarily, it was not so much the foul air, or being cooped up with hundreds of other students, as the lecturers' lack of interest in what was supposed to be their subject. Never since then have I encountered a group of people so uninspired by what they were doing as those university professors and instructors; any bank teller counting out notes that don't even belong to him, any road repairer working in the overheated air between the sun overhead and the tar boiler down below seemed more inspired. Stuffed shirts, whose voices never vibrated with the astonishment (that a good teacher's subject arouses in him), with enthusiasm, with tenderness, with self-doubt, anger, indignation, or awareness of their own ignorance, but droned incessantly on, intoned—needless to say not in the deep chest tones of Homer, but in tones of examination-oriented pedantry, interspersed now and then with a facetious undercurrent or a malicious allusion addressed to those in the know, while outside the windows green went blue and finally darkened, until the student's tiredness turned to irritation and his irritation to rage. And again as in childhood that feeling of "Let me out! Away from the lot of you in here!" But where to? Home, as in childhood? But there in my rented room, a new tiredness unknown in my childhood was to be dreaded: the tiredness of being alone in a rented room on the outskirts; solitary tiredness.

* * *

But what was to be dreaded about that? Wasn't there a bed right there in your room, along with the chair and the table?

An escape into sleep was out of the question. For one thing, that sort of tiredness brought on a paralysis in which it became virtually impossible to bend my little finger or even to bat an eyelid; my breathing seemed to stop and I froze inside and out into a pillar of tiredness. In the end, I dragged myself into bed, but after a quick fainting away from wakefulness—with no sensation of sleep— my first attempt to turn over shook me into a sleeplessness that usually went on all night. For, in my room alone, tiredness always set in late in the day, at dusk. Many others have spoken of insomnia, how it comes to dominate the insomniac's view of the world until, try as he may, he cannot help regarding existence as a calamity, all activity as pointless, and all love as absurd. The insomniac lies there waiting for the gray of dawn, which to him signifies the damnation not only of him alone in his insomniac hell but of all misbegotten humanity relegated to the wrong planet . . . I, too, have been in the world of the sleepless (and even today I still am). In early spring the first birds are heard before dawn—often enough bearing a message of Easter—but today they screech derisively at me in my cell-bed: "One-more-sleepless-night." The striking of the church clocks every quarter of an hour— even the most distant ones are quite audible—gives notice of another bad day. The bestiality at the heart of our world is manifested by the hissing and yowling of two battling tomcats. A woman's sighs or screams of so-called passion start up suddenly in the stagnant air, as though a button had been pressed, setting some mass-produced machine in motion directly above the insomniac's head, as though all our masks of affection had fallen, giving way to panic egoism (that's no loving couple, only two individuals, each bellowing his self-love) and vileness. To those frequently afflicted by episodic states of sleeplessness, if I understand their stories right, such states may form a chain of continuity and come to be regarded as permanent.

But you, who are not a sufferer from chronic insomnia: are you planning to tell us about the insomniac view of the world or that engendered by tiredness?

As might have been expected, I've started with insomnia and shall go on to the view resulting from tiredness, or rather, in the plural, I shall talk about the divergent views of the world engendered by different kinds of tiredness. How terrifying, for example, at one time, was the kind of tiredness that could crop up in the company of a woman. No, this tiredness did not crop up, it erupted like a physical cataclysm, a phenomenon of fission. And, as a matter of fact, it never confined itself to me alone, but invariably struck the woman at the same time, as though coming, like a change in the weather, from outside, from the atmosphere or from space. There we lay, stood, or sat, as though our being together were the most natural thing in the world, and then before we knew it, we were irrevocably sundered. Such a moment was always one of fright, even of horror, as in falling: "Stop! No! Don't let it happen!" But there was no help; already the two of us were irresistibly recoiling, each into his own private tiredness, not ours, but mine over here and yours over there. In this case, tiredness may have been only another name for insensibility or estrangement—but for the pressure it exerted, its effect on the environment, tiredness was the appropriate word. Even if the phenomenon occurred in a large, air-conditioned cinema. The cinema became hot and cramped. The rows of seats became crooked. The colors and the screen itself took on a sulfurous hue, then paled. When we chanced to touch each other, both our hands recoiled as from an electric shock. "In the late afternoon of the ———, a catastrophic tiredness descended out of a clear sky on the Apollo Cinema. The victims were a young couple sitting shoulder to shoulder, who were catapulted apart by a blast of tiredness. At the end of the film, which, incidentally, was entitled *About Love*, they went their separate ways without so much as a word or a glance for each other." Yes, divisive tiredness of this kind struck one mute and blind. Never in all the world could I have said to her: "I'm tired of you"—I could never have uttered the simple word "tired" (which, if we had both shouted it at once, might have set us free from our individual hells). Such tiredness destroyed our power to speak, our souls. If at least we had been able to go our separate ways. No, the effect of such tiredness was that having separated in spirit we were constrained to stay together in body. And it is quite possible that those two, possessed by the devil of tiredness, came to inspire fear.

In whom?

In each other, for one thing. Doomed to remain speechless, that sort of tiredness drove us to violence. A violence that may have expressed itself only in our manner of seeing, which distorted the other, not only as an individual, but also as a member of the other *sex.* Those ugly, ridiculous females (or males), with that innate female waddle or those incorrigible male poses. Or the violence was covert, indirect, the routine swatting of a fly, the half-absentminded rending of a flower. Or we might do something to hurt ourselves; one might chew her fingertips, the other thrust his finger into a lighted flame or punch himself in the face, while she threw herself on the ground like a baby, but without the baby's layers of protective fat. Occasionally, one of these tired individuals would indulge in physical aggression, try to shove his/her enemy or fellow prisoner out of the way, or deliver himself from her with sputtered insults. This violence seemed to be the only escape from the tiredness-couple, for once it was over, they usually managed to separate for the time being. Or tiredness gave way to exhaustion, and then at last they were able to catch their breaths and think things over. Sometimes one would come back to the other and they would stare at each other in amazement, still shaken by what had just happened, yet unable to understand it. At that point they might be able to look at each other, but with new eyes: "What could have come over us in the cinema, on the street, on the bridge?" (Once again we found a voice with which to say that, the two of us together in spite of ourselves, or the young man might speak for the young woman, or the other way around.) To that extent, a tiredness imposed on two young people might even augur a transformation—from the carefree love of the beginnings to something serious. Neither of us would have dreamed of reproaching the other with what he had just done; instead, we simultaneously opened our eyes to one of the drawbacks (irrespective of personalities) of life *à deux*, of a man's and woman's "growing" together, a drawback formerly diagnosed as "a consequence of original sin" and today as God knows what. If both succeed in escaping from this tiredness, it is to be hoped that this realization, accessible to couples who have survived a catastrophe, will enable them to stay together for the rest of their lives, and that such a tiredness will never happen to them again. And they lived together happy and contented until something else, something much less puzzling, much less to be feared, much less astonishing than that tiredness, came between them: habits, the humdrum, day-to-day business of living.

But is this divisive tiredness confined to relationships between a man and a woman? Doesn't it also intervene between friends?

No. When I felt tiredness coming on in a relationship with a friend, there was nothing catastrophic about it.

After all, we were together for only a limited time, and when that time was up, we went our separate ways, confident of remaining friends in spite of that one slack hour. Tiredness between friends was not a danger, while to young couples it was, especially if they hadn't been together for long. In love—or whatever we choose to call that feeling of fullness and wholeness—as opposed to friendship, tiredness suddenly threw everything off balance. Disenchantment: all at once the features vanished from his/her image of the other; at the end of a second of horror, he/she ceased to yield any image; the image that was there a second ago had been a mere mirage. Before you knew it, all might be over between two human beings. And the most terrifying part of it was that when this happened all seemed to be over with myself: as I saw it, I was as ugly, as insignificant as the woman with whom only a short while before I had visibly embodied a way of life ("one body and one soul"); each of us wanted him/herself as well as the accursed opposite to be demolished and wiped out on the spot. Even the things around us disintegrated into futilities: "How tired and unlived-in the express train blows by" (recollection of a line in a poem by a friend); and there was reason to fear that couple-tiredness would expand into the world-weariness, not of any particular individual, but of the universe, of the flabby leaves on the trees, of the river's suddenly sluggish flow, of the paling sky. But since such things happened only when a woman and a man were alone together, I became more and more careful as the years went by to avoid prolonged tête-à-tête situations (which was no solution, or at best a cowardly one).

But now it's time for a very different question. Isn't it just your sense of duty—because they are part of your subject—that makes you speak of the insidious, frightening varieties of tiredness—and isn't that why you seem to speak of them so clumsily, long-windedly, and, for all the exaggeration—because I can't help thinking that your story about "violent tiredness" was exaggerated if not invented—halfheartedly.

My way of speaking about malignant tiredness was worse than halfhearted; it was heartless (no, this is not a mere pun, of the kind that for its own amusement betrays an idea). But in this case I don't regard the heartlessness of my discourse as a fault. (And what's more, tiredness isn't my subject; it's my problem, a reproach that I am prepared to incur.) And in dealing with the remaining varieties of tiredness, the non-malignant, the pleasant, the delightful, which have prompted me to write this essay, I shall try to remain equally heartless, to content myself with investigating the pictures, or images, that my problem engenders in me, with making myself at home in each picture and translating it as heartlessly as possible into language with all its twists and turns and overtones. To be "in the picture" is enough for my feeling. If I dare wish for something more to help me carry on with my essay on tiredness, it will probably be a sensation: the sensation of the sun and the spring wind on Andalusian mornings in the open country outside Linares. I should like to hold it between my fingers before sitting down in my room, in the hope that this marvelous sensation between my fingers, enhanced by gusts of wind scented with wild chamomile, may carry over to the coming sentences about *good* tiredness, do them justice, and, above all, make them easier and lighter than the preceding ones. But even now I am pretty sure that tiredness is difficult. Morning after morning, the gusts of wild chamomile are more denatured by the pervasive stench of carrion; still, I shall continue, as always, to cede my right to complain about the smell to the vultures, who feed so well on the carrion. —Very well, then, on this new morning, let us rise and proceed, with more light and air between the lines, as there should be, but always close to the ground, close to the rubble between the yellowish-white chamomile flowers, with the help of the symmetry of the pictures I have known. —It is not entirely true that the only tiredness I experienced in the past was of the frightening variety. During my childhood in the late forties and fifties, the arrival of the threshing machine was still an event. The grain was not harvested automatically in the fields—by a combine that takes in the sheaves on one side, while sacks of grain all ready for the miller tumble out on the other side. No, the threshing was done in our home barn by a rented machine that went from farm to farm at harvest time. Its use required a whole chain of helpers. One of these would lift a sheaf of grain out of the farm wagon, which remained in the open because it was much too wide and piled much too high to get into the barn;

he would toss it down to the next, who would pass it on, avoiding as far as possible to lead with the "wrong," "hard-to-handle," or "ear" end, to the "big man" in the great rumbling machine which, making the entire barn tremble with its vibrations, would swing the sheaf around and push it gently between the threshing cylinders. Straw came pouring out at the back of the machine, where it formed a pile which the next helper, with a long wooden pitchfork, would pass on to the last links in the chain, the village children, as a rule all present and accounted for, who, having taken their positions in the hayloft, moved the straw into the farthermost corners, thrusting and kicking it into the last open spaces they could find, working more and more in the dark as the straw piled up around them. All this—it grew lighter in the barn as the unloading and threshing proceeded—went on without a break in a smoothly coordinated process (which, however, the slightest false move could halt or disrupt) until the wagon was empty. Even the very last link in the chain, often on the verge of suffocation toward the end of the threshing operation, wedged between two mountains of straw and unable to find room in the dark for the last handfuls thrust at him, could disrupt the whole chain by slipping away from his post. But once the threshing was happily over and the deafening machine—impossible to make yourself understood, even by shouting directly into someone's ear—switched off: What silence, not only in the barn, but throughout the countryside; and what light, enfolding rather than blinding you. While the clouds of dust settled, we gathered in the farmyard on

14

shaking knees, reeling and staggering, partly in fun. Our legs and arms were covered with scratches; we had straw in our hair, between our fingers and toes. And perhaps the most lasting effect of the day's work: the nostrils of men, women, and children alike were black, not just gray, with dust. Thus we sat—in my recollection always out of doors in the afternoon sun—savoring our common tiredness whether or not we were talking, some sitting on a bench, some on a wagon shaft, still others off on the grass of the bleaching field—the inhabitants of the whole neighborhood, regardless of generation, gathered in episodic harmony by our tiredness. A cloud of tiredness, an ethereal tiredness, held us together (while awaiting the next wagonload of sheaves). And my village childhood provided me with still other pictures of "we-tiredness."

But isn't it the past that transfigures?

If the past was of the kind that transfigures, it's all right with me. I believe in that sort of transfiguration. I know that those years were holy.

But isn't the contrast you suggest between manual work in common and solitary work on a harvest combine mere opinion and therefore suspect?

When I told you all that, it wasn't for the sake of the contrast, but of the pure picture; if such a contrast nevertheless forces itself on the reader's attention, it must mean that I haven't succeeded in communicating a pure picture.

In the following, I shall have to take greater care than ever to avoid playing one thing off, even tacitly, against another or magnifying one thing at the expense of something else, in line with the Manichaean all-good or all-bad system, which is dominant nowadays even in what used to be the most open-minded, opinion-free mode of discourse, namely storytelling: Now I'm going to tell you about the good gardeners, but only to prepare you for what I shall have to say about the wicked hunters later on. The fact is, however, that I have affecting, communicable pictures of manual workers' tiredness, but none (thus far) of a combine operator's. Then, in our shared tiredness after threshing, I saw myself for once sitting in the midst of something resembling a "people," such as I later looked for time and time again in my native Austria, and time and again failed to find. I am referring, not to the "tiredness of whole peoples," not to the tiredness that weighs on the eyelids of one late-born individual, but to the ideal tiredness that I would like to see descending on one particular small segment of the second postwar Austrian Republic, in the hope that all its groups, classes, associations, corps, and cathedral chapters may at last sit there as honestly tired as we villagers were then, all equals in our shared tiredness, united and above all purified by it. A French friend, a Jew, who was obliged to live in hiding during the German occupation, once told me, all the more movingly because his memories were transfigured by distance, that for weeks after the Liberation the whole country had been bathed in radiance, and that is how I should imagine an Austrian work-tiredness, shared by all. A criminal who has escaped scot-free may often manage to doze off, whether in a sitting or a standing position. His sleep, like that of many a fugitive, may be prolonged, deep, and stertorous, but tiredness, not to mention the tiredness that knits people together, is unknown to him; until the day when he snores his last, nothing in all the world will succeed in making him tired, unless perhaps his final punishment, for which he himself may secretly yearn. My entire country is alive with bouncy indefatigables of this breed, among them its so-called leaders; instead of joining the army of tiredness for so much as one moment, a swarming mob of habitual criminals and their accomplices, very different from those described above, of elderly but untiring mass murderers of both sexes, who throughout the country have secreted a new generation of equally tireless young fellows, who even now are training the grandchildren of the senior murderers to be secret-police agents, with the result that in this contemptible majority-country the many minorities will never be able to join forces in a community of tiredness; in this country, everyone will remain alone with his tiredness until the end of our political history. There was a time when I actually believed in the International Court of Justice, when I thought it could do something about my country (I'm not obliged to tell you how long ago that was). But that International Court seems to have gone out of existence; or, to say it in a different way: its decisions have not been put into effect within the borders of Austria and—as I have been forced to recognize since my brief moment of hope—never will be. There is no International

Court of Justice and the Austrians, I am obliged to go on believing, are the first hopelessly corrupt, totally incorrigible people in history, forever incapable of repentance or conversion.

Isn't that last assertion a mere opinion?

It is not an opinion but a picture. For what I thought I also saw. What may be opinion and therefore untrue is the word "people," for what I saw in my picture was not a "people" but the unrepentant "gang of the untired." True, this picture is contradicted by other pictures, which in the interest of fairness demand attention; but they do not penetrate as deep as the others; at the most, they offer a counterweight. My ancestors, as far back as I can trace them, were *Keuschler*, small, landless peasants; if any of them were skilled in a craft, it was carpentry. Time and again, I saw the carpenters of the region grouped together as a people of tiredness. That was in the days of the first rebuilding after the war. As the oldest of the children, I was often sent by the women of the family, my mother, my grandmother, and my sister-in-law, to deliver warm lunch pails to the construction workers in the area. All the men in the family who had not been killed in the war, even for a time my sixty-year-old grandfather, worked there with other carpenters putting up roofs. In my picture they sit eating their lunch not far from the frame of a house—once again that special way of sitting!—on rough-hewn beams or on peeled but not yet planed tree trunks. They have taken their hats off, and their foreheads with the hair plastered to them look milky white in contrast to their dark faces. All seem sinewy, fine-boned, and sparely built, I can't recall a single pot-bellied carpenter. They eat slowly and in silence; even my German stepfather, the "carpenter's helper," who could only hold his own in the strange country and the unfamiliar village environment with the help of his big-city bluster (may he rest in peace). After the meal they sat awhile, gently tired, talking, without jokes, without complaining, without raising their voices, mostly about their families, sometimes quietly about the weather, until in the end their work arrangements for the afternoon crowded out all other topics. Though there actually was a foreman, I had the impression that none of these workers dominated or commanded; this in a way was part of their tiredness. And yet, despite their heavy, inflamed eyelids —typical of that kind of tiredness—all were wide awake, each one of them was presence of mind personified ("Here it comes!" An apple is tossed. "Got it!") and lively (time and again, several at once would spontaneously burst into a telling of stories: "Before the war, when Mother was still alive, we'd go and see her at the hospital in Sankt Veit, and that night we'd hike back home, a good fifty kilometers, by way of the Trixen Valley . . ."). The colors and shapes of my pictures of the fragmentary community of tiredness are the blue of work denims, the straight red marks that the guideline slaps on the beams, the red-and-violet of oval-shaped carpenter's pencils, the yellow of yardsticks, the oval of the air bubble in the spirit level. By now the sweaty hair on our temples had dried and

fluffed up; the hats, which have been put back on, are
free from badges, and pencils rather than chamois beards
have been stuck in the bands. If transistor radios had
existed in those days, I'm pretty certain they'd have stayed
away from those building sites. Yet a kind of music seems
to reach me from there—the music of clairaudient tiredness. Not to forget the way those places looked; again I
say: it was a holy time—episodes of holiness. I myself, of
course, was not one of those tired people (as I had been
one among the servants of the threshing machine) and I
envy them. But when later, in my adolescence, I might
have been one of them, it became a very different matter
from what it had been in the imagination of the lunch-
pail carrier. When my grandmother died and my grandfather was pensioned and gave up farming, the great
household community of the generations—others in the
village as well as ours—went out of existence. My parents
built a house of their own, and everyone in the family,
down to the smallest child, had to help with the building.
For me, too, a job was found, and I learned an entirely
new kind of tiredness. My work in the early stages consisted largely of pushing a wheelbarrow loaded with stone
blocks uphill to the building site, which was inaccessible
to trucks, over a plank walk that had been laid over mud.
I no longer saw it as work done by us all in common,
but as sheer drudgery. The effort of pushing those loads
uphill from morning till night took so much out of me
that I no longer had eyes for the things around me, and
could only stare straight ahead at the jagged gray stones
I was hauling, at the gray streams of cement that came

rolling down the path, and above all at the joints between planks, which regularly forced me to lift or tilt the barrow slightly on the corners and curves. Often enough, when we came to these gaps, my wheelbarrow capsized, and I with it. Those weeks taught me what forced labor or slavery might be. At the end of the day, I was "wrecked," as the peasants put it; my hands were bruised and my toes burned by the concrete that had oozed between them. Destroyed by tiredness, I would flop (rather than sit) down. Unable to swallow, I could neither eat nor speak. This particular tiredness—and that may have been its special characteristic—seemed to be terminal; one would never get over it. I fell asleep the moment I lay down, and awoke in the gray of dawn, when it was almost time for work, more exhausted than ever, as though the cruel drudgery had cleaned me out of everything that might have contributed to the most elementary sense of being alive—the feel of the early light, the wind on my temples—as though there would never be an end to this living death. Until then, when confronted by unpleasant chores, I had always been quick to think up dodges and evasions. Now I was even too worn out to shirk in my old familiar ways: "I have to study; there's an exam coming up"; "I'm going to the woods to gather mushrooms for all of you." In any case, nothing I could say would do a particle of good. Though, come to think of it, I was working for my own benefit—our house—my tiredness was invariably that of a hired hand, an isolating tiredness. Of course there were other jobs that were equally dreaded by just about everyone, such as digging ditches for water pipes: "This job is a bitch, a devil!" But oddly enough, my dead-tiredness lifted in time, giving way, to "carpenter-tiredness"? No, to a feeling of sportsmanship, to a Stakhanovite ambition, combined with a kind of gallows humor. I experienced still another kind of tiredness in my student days while working the morning shift—from early morning to early afternoon—in the shipping room of a department store during the Christmas and Easter rush, to make a little money. I'd get up at four to catch the first streetcar, urinate into an empty jam jar in my room so as not to disturb the landlady, and leave the house unwashed. The work was done by artificial light on the top floor of the building; it consisted of dismembering old cartons and with a gigantic guillotine cutting out enormous rectangles that would be used to reinforce the new cartons being packed in the adjoining room. In the long run, this activity, like chopping or sawing wood at home, did me good by leaving my thoughts free but, thanks to the steady rhythm, not too free. The new tiredness made itself felt when we stepped out into the street and separated after the shift. Alone in my tiredness, blinking, my glasses coated with dust, my open shirt collar soiled and rumpled, I suddenly had new eyes for the familiar street scene. I no longer saw myself as one with all these people who were going somewhere—to the stores, the railroad station, the movies, the university. Though wakefully tired, neither sleepy nor self-absorbed, I felt excluded from society—an eerie feeling. Moving in the opposite direction from all these other people, I was headed nowhere. I entered a lecture hall with the feeling that this was a forbidden room, and I found it even harder than usual to listen to that droning voice; what was being said wasn't meant for me, I hadn't even the status of a "special student." Every day I longed more and more to be back with the tired little group of morning-shift workers up in the loft, and today, when I try to recapture the picture, I realize that even then, when I was very young, only nineteen or twenty, long before I seriously took up writing, I ceased to feel like a student among students—an unpleasant, rather frightening feeling.

But isn't there something vaguely romantic about the way you derive all your pictures of tiredness from farmhands and manual laborers, and never from the upper or lower middle class?

I've never come in contact with a picturable tiredness among the middle class.

Can't you at least imagine one?

No. It seems to me that tiredness just isn't right for them; they regard it as a kind of misbehavior, like going barefoot. What's more, they can't supply an image of tiredness, because their activities don't lend themselves to that kind of thing. The most they can do is look "weary unto death" at the end, but we can all manage that, I hope. Nor am I able to visualize the tiredness of the rich and powerful, with the possible exception of deposed kings, such as

Oedipus and Lear. On the other hand, I can't conceive of fully automated factories disgorging tired workers at closing time. I see only big, imperious-looking louts with smug faces and great flabby hands, who will hurry off to the nearest slot-machine establishment and carry on with their blissfully mindless manipulations. (I know what you're going to say now: "Before talking like that, you yourself should get good and tired, just for the sake of fairness." But there are times when I have to be unfair, when I want to be unfair. Anyway, I'm good and tired already from chasing after images, as you accuse me of doing.) Later on, I came to know still another kind of tiredness, comparable to what I experienced in the shipping room; that was when I finally started writing in earnest, day after day for months at a time—there was no other way out. Once again, when I went out into the city streets after the day's work, it seemed to me that I had lost my connection with all the people around me. But the way I felt about this loss of connection wasn't the same anymore. It no longer mattered to me that I had ceased to be a participant in normal everyday life; on the contrary, in my tiredness verging on exhaustion, my non-participation gave me an altogether pleasant feeling. No longer was society inaccessible to me; I, on the contrary, was now inaccessible to society and everyone in it. What are your entertainments, your festivities, your hugging and kissing to me? I had the trees, the grass, the movie screen on which Robert Mitchum displayed his inscrutable pantomime for me alone, and I had the jukebox on which, for me alone, Bob Dylan sang his "Sad-eyed Lady of the

Lowlands," or Ray Davies his and my "I'm Not Like Everybody Else."

Wasn't that sort of tiredness likely to degenerate into arrogance?

Yes, I'd often, in looking myself over, surprise a cold, misanthropic arrogance or, worse, a condescending pity for all the commonplace occupations that could never in all the world lead to a royal tiredness such as mine. In the hours after writing, I was an "untouchable," enthroned, so to speak, regardless of where I happened to be: "Don't touch me!" And if in the pride of my tiredness I nevertheless let myself be touched, it might just as well have never happened. It wasn't until much later that I came to know tiredness as a becoming-accessible, as the possibility of being touched and of being able to touch in turn. This happened very rarely—only great events can happen so rarely—and hasn't recurred for a long while, as though such miracles were confined to a certain segment of human existence and could be repeated only in exceptional situations, a war, a natural catastrophe, or some other time of trouble. On the few occasions when I have been—but what verb goes with it?—"favored"? "struck?" with such tiredness, I was indeed going through a period of personal distress, during which, fortunately for me, I met someone who was in a similar state. This other person always proved to be a woman. Our distress was not enough to bind us; it also took an erotic tiredness after a hardship suffered together. There seems to be a rule that before a man and a woman can become a dream couple for some hours at a time they must have a long, arduous journey behind them, must have met in a place foreign to them both and as far as possible from any sort of home or hominess, and must have confronted a danger, or perhaps only a long period of bewilderment in the midst of the enemy country, which can also be one's own. This tiredness, in a place of refuge that has suddenly become quiet, may suddenly give these two, a man and a woman, to each other with a naturalness and fervor unknown in other unions, however loving; what happens then is "like an exchange of bread and wine," as another friend put it. Sometimes when I try to communicate the feeling of such a union in tiredness, a line from a poem comes to mind: "Words of love—each one of them laughing . . ." which isn't far from the "one body and one soul" cited above, though in that case both bodies were steeped in silence; or I would simply vary the words spoken in a Hitchcock film by a tipsy Ingrid Bergman while fondling the tired and (still) rather remote Cary Grant: "Forget it—a tired man and a drunken woman—that won't add up to much of a couple." My variation: "A tired man and a tired woman—what a glorious couple that will be." Or "with you" appears as a single word, like the Spanish *contigo* . . . or in German (or English), perhaps instead of saying: "I'm tired of you," one might say: "I'm tired with you." In the light of these extraordinary findings, I see Don Juan not as a seducer but as a perpetually tired hero who can be counted on to be overcome by tiredness at the right time in the company of a tired woman, the consequence being that all women fall into his arms, but never waste a tear on him once the mysteries of erotic tiredness have been enacted; for what has happened between those two will have been for all time: two such people know of nothing more enduring than this one entwinement, neither feels the need of a repetition; in fact, both dread the thought. That's all very well, but how does this Don Juan bring on his forever new tiredness, which makes him and his mistress so wonderfully ready to succumb? Not only one or two but a thousand and three such simultaneities which, down to the tiniest patch of skin, engrave themselves forever on this pair of bodies, each and every impulse being genuine, unmistakable, congruent, and of course spontaneous. In any case, you and I, after such ecstasies of tiredness, would be lost to the usual bodily fuss and bother.

What did you have left when it was over?

Even greater tirednesses.

Are there, in your opinion, even greater tirednesses than those already referred to?

More than ten years ago, I took a night flight from Anchorage, Alaska, to New York. It was a long haul from Cook Inlet, great ice floes rushing in at low tide and galloping back into the ocean at low tide, a stopover amid snow flurries in the gray of dawn in Edmonton, Canada, another in Chicago after much circling around the airfield

and waiting in line on the runway under the harsh morning sun, to the final landing in the sultry afternoon, miles
out of New York. Arriving at the hotel, I felt ill, cut off
from the world after a night without sleep, air, or exercise,
and wanted to go straight to bed. But then I saw the
streets along Central Park in the early-autumn sunlight.
People seemed to be strolling about, as though on a holiday. I wanted to be with them and felt I'd be missing
something if I stayed in my room. Still dazed and alarm-
ingly wobbly from loss of sleep, I found a place on a sunlit
café terrace, with clamor and gasoline fumes all around
me. But then, I don't remember how, whether little by
little or all at once, came transformation. I once read that
depressives can be cured by being kept awake night after
night; this "treatment" seemed to stabilize the fearsomely
swaying "suspension bridge of the ego." I had that image
before me when the torment of my tiredness began to
lift. This tiredness had something of a recovery about it.
Hadn't I heard people talk about "fighting off tiredness"?
For me the fight was over. Now tiredness was my friend.
I was back in the world again and even—though not
because this was Manhattan—in its center. But there were
other things, many, in fact, one more enchanting than the
last. Until late that night I did nothing but sit and look;
it was almost as if I had no need to draw breath. No
spectacular breathing exercises or yoga contortions. You
just sit and breathe more or less correctly in the light of
your tiredness. Lots of beautiful women passed, sometimes
an incredible number, from time to time their beauty
brought tears to my eyes—and all, as they passed, took

notice of me. I existed. (Strange that my look of tiredness was especially acknowledged by the beautiful women, but also by children and a few old men.) Neither they nor I thought of going any further and trying to strike up an acquaintance. I wanted nothing from them; just being able to look at them was enough for me. My gaze was indeed that of a good spectator at a game that cannot be successful without at least one such onlooker. This tired man's looking-on was an activity, it did something, it played a part; because of it, the actors in the play became better, more beautiful than ever—for one thing because while being looked at by eyes such as mine they took their time. As by a miracle, the tiredness of such an onlooker nullified his ego, that eternal creator of unrest, and with it all other distortions, quirks, and frowns; nothing remained but his candid eyes, at least as inscrutable as Robert Mitchum's. The action of this selfless onlooker encompassed far more than the beautiful female passersby and drew everything that lived and moved into its world-center. My tiredness articulated the muddle of crude perception, not by breaking it up, but by making its components recognizable, and with the help of rhythms endowed it with form—form as far as the eye could see—a vast horizon of tiredness.

But the scenes of violence, the clashes, the screams—did they become friendly forms on the vast horizon?

I have been speaking here of tiredness in peacetime, in the present interim period. In those hours there was peace, in the Central Park area as elsewhere. And the astonishing part of it was that my tiredness seemed to participate in this momentary peace, for my gaze disarmed every intimation of a violent gesture, a conflict, or even of an unfriendly attitude, before it could get started—this by virtue of a compassion very different from the occasional contemptuous pity that comes of creative tiredness: call it sympathy as understanding.

But what was so unusual about that gaze? Its special character?

I saw—and the other saw that I saw—his object at the same time as he did: the trees under which he was walking, the book he held in his hand, the light in which he was standing, even if it was the artificial light of a store; the old fop *along with* this light-colored suit and the carnation he was holding; the salesman *along with* his heavy suitcase; the giant *along with* the invisible child on his shoulders; myself *along with* the leaves blowing out of the park; and every one of us *along with* the sky overhead.

Suppose there was no such object?

Then my tiredness created it, and in a twinkling the other, who a moment ago had still been wandering about in the void, felt surrounded by the aura of his object . . . And that's not all. Because of my tiredness, the thousands of unconnected happenings all about me arranged themselves into an order that was more than form; each one

entered into me as the precisely fitting part of a finely
attuned, light-textured story; and its events told themselves without the mediation of words. Thanks to my
tiredness, the world cast off its names and became great.
I have a rough picture of four possible attitudes of my
linguistic self to the world: in the first, I am mute, cruelly
excluded from events; in the second, the confusion of
voices, of talk, passes from outside into my inner self,
though I am still as mute as before, capable at the most
of screaming; in the third, finally, life enters into me by
beginning spontaneously, sentence for sentence, to tell
stories, usually to a definite person, a child, a friend; and
finally, in the fourth, which I experienced most lastingly
in that day's clear-sighted tiredness, the world tells its
own story without words, in utter silence, to me as well
as to that gray-haired onlooker over there and to that
magnificent woman who is striding by; all peaceable happening was itself a story, and unlike wars and battles,
which need a poet or a chronicler before they can take
shape, these stories shaped themselves in my tired eyes
into an epic and, moreover, as then became apparent to
me, an ideal epic. The images of the fugitive world
meshed one with another, and took form.

Ideal?

Yes, ideal: because in this epic everything that happened
was right; things kept happening, yet there was not too
much or too little of anything. All that's needed for an
epic is a world, a history of mankind, that tells itself as

it should be. Utopian? The other day I read here on a poster: "La utopia no existe," which might be translated as "The no-place does not exist." Just give that a thought and history will start moving. In any case, my utopian tiredness of that day was connected with at least one place. That day I felt much more sense of place than usual. It was as though, no sooner arrived, I in my tiredness had taken on the smell of the place; I was an old inhabitant. And in similar spells of tiredness during the years that followed, still more associations attached themselves to that place. Total strangers spoke to me, perhaps because I looked familiar to them, or perhaps for no particular reason. In Edinburgh, where after looking for hours at Poussin's *Seven Sacraments*, which at last showed Baptism, the Lord's Supper, and the rest in the proper perspective, I sat radiant with tiredness in an Italian restaurant, feeling self-conscious about being waited on—an exceptional state related to my tiredness; all the waiters agreed that they had seen me before, though each in a different place, one in Santorin (where I have never been), another last summer with a sleeping bag on Lake Garda—neither the sleeping bag nor the lake was right. In the train from Zurich to Biel after staying up all night celebrating the end of the children's school year, I was sitting opposite a young woman who had spent an equally sleepless night at a party celebrating the end of the Tour de Suisse bicycle race. On the instructions of the bank she worked for, which had co-sponsored the Tour, she had performed the duties of a hostess, distributing flowers and kisses to each prizewinner as he stepped forward . . . Her story came tumbling out of the tired woman as spontaneously as if we had known everything else about each other. One racer, who had won twice in a row and was rewarded with a second kiss, was so engrossed in his sporting prowess that he no longer recognized her, as she told me cheerfully, admiringly, and without a trace of disappointment. In addition to being tired, she was hungry, and she wasn't going to bed, she was going to eat lunch with her girlfriend in Biel. There, I realized, was another explanation for her unsuspecting trustfulness: in addition to her tiredness, her hunger. The tiredness of the well fed can't manage that. "We were hungry and tired," says the young woman in Dashiell Hammett's *The Glass Key* in telling Sam Spade her dream about the two of them: what brought them together, then and later, was hunger and tiredness. It seems to me that apart from children—the way they turn around and stare expectantly at the man sitting there—and other tired people, idiots and animals are most receptive to such tiredness. A few days ago an idiot here in Linares, hopping along absently hand in hand with a member of his family, seemed as startled at the sight of me, sitting on a bench exhausted by my literary efforts of the morning and afternoon, as if he had taken me for a fellow idiot or something even more amazing. Not only his Mongoloid eyes but his whole face beamed at me; he stopped still and had to be literally dragged away—his features expressing pure pleasure, simply because someone had seen him and acknowledged his existence. And this was not a unique occurrence. In many a time and place the idiots of the world, European, Arab,

Japanese, presenting the drama of themselves with child-like pleasure, have been drawn into this tired idiot's field of vision. Once in Friuli, not far from the village of Medea, when exhausted after completing a piece of work and walking for hours across the treeless plain, I came to the edge of a forest and saw two ducks, a deer, and a hare lying together in the grass. Catching sight of me, they seemed about to take flight, but then resumed their even rhythm; pulling up grass, browsing, waddling about. On the road near the Poblet monastery in Catalonia I fell in with two dogs, a big one and a small one, who may have been father and son. They joined up with me, sometimes following me, sometimes running on ahead. I was so tired that I forgot my usual fear of dogs, and besides, or so I imagined, my long wanderings in the region must have steeped me in its smell, so the dogs took me for granted. True enough, they began to play, the "father" describing circles around me and the "son" chasing him between my legs. Great, I thought. Here I have an image of true human tiredness: it creates openings, making room for an epic that will encompass all beings, now including the animals. Here perhaps a digression may be in order. In the chamomile-scented rubble outside Linares, where I go for a walk each day, I have observed very different interactions among human beings and animals. I can speak of them only in shorthand. Those scattered forms apparently resting in the shadows of the ruins or stone blocks but actually lying in ambush, within gunshot of the little cages fastened to flexible poles planted in the rubble. Cages so tiny that the fluttering of the inmates makes them sway,

thus offering larger birds an alluring mobile bait. (But
the shadow of the eagle is far away, sweeping across my
paper as I sit in my eerily quiet eucalyptus grove hard by
the ruins of the lead mine, my open-air studio during the
ecstatic bellowing and trumpeting of the Spanish Easter
Week); —or those excited children running out of the
gypsy encampment on the heath, a sleek noble-headed
dog frolicking around them, yelping with eagerness at
the sight of the spectacle organized by a boy-almost-man:
hare let loose on the savanna, dog speeding in pursuit,
hare twisting, turning, and doubling back, but soon
caught, dropped, caught again more quickly than before,
flung this way and that in the dog's jaws. Dog racing
across field, hare squeaking interminably, show ending
with return of children to camp, dog jumping up, ring-
leader boy holding out hand, grabbing hare by ears; the
hare wet with blood, still twitching a little, its paws go
limp; its little face, seen in profile, held high above the
children's heads, utterly helpless and forlorn, more
sublime than the face of any animal or human being, leads
the procession into the sunset. —Or only the other day,
as I was on my way home to town from writing in the
eucalyptus grove, a crowd of teenagers by the stone wall
around the olive field, brandishing olive branches and
reeds, shouting, running forward and back, pushing and
kicking at a pile of stones, and from under the stones,
now visible in the sunlight, a long, thick, coiled snake, at
first barely moving, just the twitching of the head and
the darting of the tongue—still heavy with winter sleep?
Reeds raining down from all sides, splintering yet lethal;

the assailants, hardly more than children, myself among them as I remember it, still howling and rushing back and forth; at last the snake rearing to full height yet cutting a pathetic figure, in no position to attack, not even threatening, just mechanically executing the hereditary gesture of the snake, and thus upraised in profile, with head crushed and blood flowing from its mouth, suddenly, just before collapsing under the shower of stones like the hare, a third figure, something like the one that appears for a moment at the back of the stage while the curtain, painted with the usual human and animal forms, rises. But why do I persist in telling and retelling such horrors, which communicate no story but at the most lend confirmation, while what my unifying tirednesses have to tell me calls forth again and again a natural stretching out which induces an epic breathing.

That's all very well, but don't you realize that those horrors were not mere horrors. Look at it this way. You were just going to record them, but in spite of yourself you were very nearly drawn into storytelling, and if in the end you avoided its verb form, the historical past, it was only by a deliberate trick. And besides, your horror stories are more colorful, or in any case more suggestive, than the infinitely peaceful incidents of your epic tiredness?

But I'm not interested in suggestiveness. I have no desire to persuade, not even with images. I only want to remind each one of you of his own very narrative tiredness. And its visual quality will soon become apparent, at the end of this essay—right now if I've become tired enough in the meantime.

But quite aside from your anecdotes and fragmentary glimpses, what is the essence of the ultimate tiredness? How does it work? What good is it? Does it enable a tired person to act?

It is itself the best action, because it is in itself a beginning, a doing, a getting under way, so to speak. This getting under way is a lesson. Tiredness provides teachings that can be applied. What, you may ask, does it teach? The history of ideas used to operate with the concept of the "Thing in itself"; no longer, for an object can never be manifested "in itself," but only in relation to me. But the tirednesses that I have in mind renew the old concept and give it meaning for me. What's more: they give me the idea along with the concept. And better still, with the idea of the thing, I possess, almost palpably, a law: The thing not only is, but *should* be just as it appears at the moment. And furthermore: in such fundamental tiredness, the thing is never manifested alone but always in conjunction with other things, and even if there are not very many, they will all be together in the end. "And now even the dog with its barking says: All together!" And in conclusion: such tirednesses demand to be shared.

Why so philosophical all of a sudden?

.   .   .

Right—maybe I'm not tired enough. In the hour of the ultimate tiredness, there's no room for philosophical questions. Time is also space, and space-time is also history. Being is also becoming. The other becomes I. Those two children down there before my tired eyes are also I. And the way the older sister is dragging her little brother through the room has a meaning and a value, and nothing is worth more than anything else—the rain falling on the tired man's wrist is worth as much as his view of the people walking on the other side of the river, both are good and beautiful, and that is as it should be, now and forever—and above all it is true. How the sister-I grabs me, the brother, by the waist—that is true. And in the tired look, the relative is seen as absolute and the part as the whole.

What becomes of perception?

I have an image for the "all in one": those seventeenth-century, for the most part Dutch floral, still lifes, in which a beetle, a snail, a bee, or a butterfly sits true to life, in the flowers, and although none of these may suspect the presence of the others, they are all there together at the moment, *my* moment.

Couldn't you try to express yourself concretely and not indirectly through historical images?

Very well; then sit down—I hope you've become tired enough by now—with me on that stone wall at the edge of the dirt road, or better still, because we'll be closer to the ground, squat down with me on the strip of grass in the middle of the road. See how all at once, with the help of this colored reflection, the world-map of the "all together" is revealed. Close to the earth, we are at the same time far enough away to see the rearing caterpillar, the beetle boring into the sand, and the ant hobbling over an olive at the same time as the strip of bark rolled into a figure eight before our eyes.

Not an illustrated report; tell me a story.

A few days ago the dead body of a mole was making its way through the dust of this Andalusian road as slowly and solemnly as the statues of sorrow that are carried about on stands during Easter Week here in Andalusia; under it, when I turned it over, there was a procession of glittering-gold carrion beetles. And last winter, on a similar dirt road in the Pyrenees, I squatted down in the exact same way as we are squatting now, and watched the snow falling in small grainy flakes, but, once it lay on the ground, indistinguishable from grains of light-colored sand; in melting, however, it left strange puddles, dark spots very different from those made by raindrops, much larger and more irregular as they trickled away into the dust. And as a child, at just the same distance from the ground as we are now, I was walking in the first morning light with my grandfather, on just such a dirt road in Austria, barefoot, just as close to the ground and just as infinitely far from the dispersed craters in the dust, where the raindrops had struck—my first image, one that will let itself be repeated forever.

At last your metaphors for the effects of tiredness introduce not only small-sized objects but also human measure. But why is the tired individual always you and no one else?

It always seemed to me that my greatest tirednesses were also ours. Late one night in Dutovlje in the Karst, the old men were standing at the bar. I had been at odds with them. Tiredness tells its story through the other, even if I've never heard of him. Those two over there with the slicked-down hair, the gaunt faces, the split nails, and fresh shirts are farm workers, *labradores*, who have worked hard all day in the wilds and have come a long way on foot to the town bar, unlike all the others who are standing around here; the one over there, for instance, wolfing down his meal all alone, is a stranger to the region, whose home office has sent him to the Land Rover assembly plant in Linares far from his family, and the old man who can be seen day after day standing at the edge of the olive field, a little dog at his feet, his elbows propped on a fork of the tree, grieving for his dead wife. "Fantasy" comes to the ideally tired man but is different from the fantasy of the sleepers in the Bible or the *Odyssey*, who have visions: without visions his fantasy shows him what is. And now, though not tired, I have the gall to tell you my fantasy of the last stage of tiredness. In this stage the tired god sat tired and feeble in his tiredness, but—just a notch tireder than a tired human had ever been—all-seeing, with a gaze which, if acknowledged and accepted by those seen, regardless of where in the cosmos, would exert a kind of power.

That's enough about stages! Speak to me for once about the tiredness you're thinking of, just as your thoughts come to you, in confusion.

Thanks! Such confusion is at present just the thing for me and my problem. So let's have a Pindaric ode, not to a victor but to a tired man. I conceive of the Pentecostal company that received the Holy Ghost as tired to a man. The inspiration of tiredness tells them not so much what should, as what need not, be. Tiredness is the angel who touches the fingers of the one dreaming king, while the other kings go on sleeping dreamlessly. Healthy tiredness is in itself recovery. A certain tired man can be seen as a new Orpheus; the wildest beasts gather around him and are at last able to join in his tiredness. Tiredness gives dispersed individuals the keynote. The more sleepless nights he lived though, the more brilliantly the private eye Philip Marlowe succeeded in solving his cases. The tired Odysseus won the love of Nausicaä. Tiredness makes you younger than you ever have been. Tiredness is greater than the self. Everything becomes extraordinary in the tranquillity of tiredness—how extraordinary, for instance, is the bundle of paper which the astonishingly easygoing man over there is carrying across the astonishingly quiet Calle Cervantes. Epitome of tiredness. On Easter Eve long ago, at the commemoration of the Resurrection, the old men of the village used to lie prone before the tomb, wearing red brocade cloaks instead of their blue work clothes, the sunburned skin of their necks split into a polygonal design by their lifelong exertions; the dying grandmother in her quiet tiredness appeased the whole household, even her incorrigibly choleric husband; and every evening here in Linares I watched the growing tiredness of the many small children who had been dragged to the bars: no more greed, no grabbing hold of things, only playfulness. And with all that, is there still any need to say that even in low-level images of tiredness distinctions are preserved?

All very well and good; undeniably, your problem is concrete enough (despite the typically mystical stammering in your way of expressing it). But how are such tirednesses to be induced? By artificially keeping yourself awake? By means of long-distance flights? Forced marches? Herculean labors? By experimenting with dying? Have you a recipe for your utopia? Pep pills for the entire population? Or powders to be added to the drinking water in the Land of the Untired?

I know of no recipe, not even for myself. All I know is this: Such tiredness cannot be planned, cannot be taken as an aim. But I also know that it never sets in without a cause, but always after a hardship, a difficulty needed to be surmounted. And now let us rise and go out into the streets, among people, to see whether a little shared tiredness may not be waiting for us and what it may have to tell us?

But does real tiredness, or real asking for that matter, imply standing rather than sitting? Remember that gnarled old woman, harassed as usual by her son, who was always in a rush in spite of his gray hair, and how she pleaded: "Oh, let's just *sit* here a little longer."

Yes, let's sit, but not here in this lonely place, amid the rustling eucalyptus leaves, but on the edge of the boulevards, the *avenidas*, looking on, perhaps with a jukebox within reach.

You won't find a jukebox in all Spain.

There's one right here in Linares, a very strange one.

Tell me about it.

No. Another time. In an Essay on the Jukebox. Perhaps.

But before we go out into the street, one last image of tiredness.

All right. It is also my last image of mankind, reconciled in its very last moments, in cosmic tiredness.

Postscript
Those little bird cages in the savanna were not put there
to attract eagles. In answer to my question, a man sitting
at some distance from one of these rectangles told me he
moved them out into the rubble field because he wanted
to hear the little birds singing; and the olive branches
thrust into the ground beside the cages were not intended
to lure the eagles out of the sky, but to make the siskins
sing.

Second postscript
Or do the siskins hop for the eagle up there in the sky
—which the people would like to see swooping down for
a change?

Linares, Andalusia
March 1989

ESSAY

ON

THE

JUKEBOX

Translated by

Krishna Winston

Dar tiempo al tiempo.
—SPANISH SAYING

And I saw her standing there.
—LENNON / MCCARTNEY

Intending to make a start at last on a long-planned essay
on the jukebox, he bought a ticket to Soria at the bus
station in Burgos. The departure gates were in a roofed
inner courtyard; that morning, when several buses were
leaving at the same time for Madrid, Barcelona, and Bil-
bao, they had been thronged; now, in early afternoon,
only the bus for Soria was parked there in the semicircle
with a couple of passengers, presumably traveling alone,
its baggage compartment open and almost empty. When
he turned over his suitcase to the driver—or was it the
conductor?—standing outside, the man said "Soria!" and
touched him lightly on the shoulder. The traveler wanted
to take in a bit more of the locale, and walked back and
forth on the platform until the engine was started. The
woman selling lottery tickets, who that morning had been
working the crowd like a gypsy, was no longer to be seen
in the deserted station. He pictured her having a meal
somewhere near the indoor market of Burgos, on the
table a glass of dark-red wine and the bundle of tickets
for the Christmas lottery. On the asphalt of the platform
was a large sooty spot; the tailpipe of a since vanished
bus must have puffed exhaust there for a long time, so
thick was the black layer crisscrossed by the prints of

many different shoe soles and suitcase wheels. He, too, now crossed this spot, for the specific purpose of adding his own shoe prints to the others, as if by so doing he could produce a good omen for his proposed undertaking. The strange thing was that on the one hand he was trying to convince himself that this "Essay on the Jukebox" was something inconsequential or casual, while on the other hand he was feeling the usual apprehension that overcame him before writing, and involuntarily sought refuge in favorable signs and portents—even though he did not trust them for a moment, but rather, as now, promptly forbade himself to do so, reminding himself of a comment on superstition in the *Characters* of Theophrastus, which he was reading on this trip: superstition was a sort of cowardice in the face of the divine. But, even so, the prints of these many and different shoes, including their various trademarks, layered on top of each other, white on black, and disappearing outside the circle of soot, were an image he could take with him as he continued his journey.

That he would buckle down to the "Essay on the Jukebox" in Soria had been planned for some time. It was now the beginning of December, and the previous spring, while flying over Spain, he had come upon an article in the airline magazine that featured this remote town in the Castilian highlands. Because of its location, far from any major routes, and almost bypassed by history for nearly a millennium, Soria was the quietest and most secluded town on the entire peninsula; in the center of town and also outside of town, standing by themselves in a desolate area, were several Romanesque structures, complete with well-preserved sculptures. Despite its smallness, the town of Soria was the capital of the province of the same name. In the early twentieth century Soria had been home to a man who, as a French teacher, then as a young husband, then almost immediately as a widower, had captured the region in his poems with a wealth of precise detail, the poet Antonio Machado. Soria, at an altitude of more than a thousand meters above sea level, was lapped at its foundations by the headwaters of the Duero, here very slow-moving, along whose banks—past the poplars that Machado called "singing" (*álamos cantadores*) because of the nightingales, *ruiseñores*, in their dense branches, and between cliffs that repeatedly narrowed to form canyons—according to the appropriately illustrated article, paths led far out into the untouched countryside . . .

With this "Essay on the Jukebox" he intended to articulate the significance this object had had in the different phases of his life, now that he was no longer young. Yet hardly any of his acquaintances had had anything to say when, in the last few months, he had embarked on a sort of playful market research and had asked them what they knew about this piece of machinery. Some, including, to be sure, a priest, had merely shrugged their shoulders and shaken their heads at the suggestion that such a thing could be of any interest. Others thought the jukebox was a kind of pinball machine, while still others were not even familiar with the word and had no idea what was meant until it was described as a "music box" or "music cabinet."

Precisely such ignorance, such indifference stimulated him all the more—after the initial disappointment at finding, yet again, that not everyone shared his experiences—to take on this object, or this subject matter, especially since it seemed that in most countries and places the time of jukeboxes was pretty much past (he, too, was perhaps gradually getting beyond the age for standing in front of these machines and pushing the buttons).

Of course he had also read the so-called literature on jukeboxes, though intending to forget most of it on the spot; what would count when he began writing was primarily his own observations. In any case, there was little written on the topic. The authoritative work, at least up to now, was probably the *Complete Identification Guide to the Wurlitzer Jukeboxes*, published in 1984 in Des Moines, far off in the American Midwest. Author: Rick Botts. This is more or less what the reader recalled of the history of the jukebox: it was during Prohibition in the United States, in the twenties, that in the back-door taverns, the "speakeasies," automatic music players were first installed. The derivation of the term "jukebox" was uncertain, whether from "jute" or from the verb "to jook," which was supposed to be African in origin and meant "to dance." In any case, the blacks used to gather after working in the jute fields of the South at so-called jute joints or juke joints, where they could put a nickel in the slot of the automatic music player and hear Billie Holiday, Jelly Roll Morton, or Louis Armstrong, musicians whom the radio stations, all owned by whites, did not play. The golden age of the jukebox began when Prohibition was lifted in the thirties, and bars sprang up everywhere; even in establishments like tobacco stores and beauty parlors there were automatic record players, because of space limitations no larger than the cash register and located next to it on the counter. This flowering ended, for the time being, with the Second World War, when the materials used to make jukeboxes were rationed—primarily plastic and steel. Wood replaced the metal parts, and then, in the middle of the war, all production was converted to armaments. The leading manufacturers of jukeboxes, Wurlitzer and Seeburg, now produced de-icing units for airplanes and electromechanical components.

The form of the music boxes was a story in itself. Through its form, the jukebox was supposed to stand out "from its not always very colorful surroundings." The most important man in the company was therefore the designer; while the basic structure for a Wurlitzer was a rounded arch, Seeburg as a rule used rectangular cases with domes on top. The principle seemed to be that each new model could deviate from the previous one only so much, so that it was still recognizable. This principle was so firmly established that a particularly innovative jukebox, shaped like an obelisk, topped not by a head or a flame but by a dish containing the speaker, which propelled the music up toward the ceiling, proved a complete failure. Accordingly, variation was confined almost exclusively to the lighting effects or to components of the frame: a peacock in the middle of the box, in constantly changing colors; plastic surfaces, previously simply colored, now marbled; decorative moldings, once fake bronze, now chromed; arched frames, now in the form of transparent neon tubes, filled with large and small bubbles in constant motion, "signed Paul Fuller"—at this point the reader and observer of this history of design finally learned the name of its main hero and realized that he had always unconsciously wanted to know it, ever since he had first been overcome with amazement at encountering one of these mighty objects glowing in all the colors of the rainbow in some dim back room.

The bus ride from Burgos to Soria went east across the almost deserted *meseta*. Even with all the empty seats, it seemed as though there were more people together on the bus than anywhere outside in those barren highlands. The sky was gray and drizzly, the few fields between cliffs and clay lay fallow. With a solemn face and dreamy, wide-open eyes, a young girl ceaselessly cracked and chewed sunflower seeds, something often seen in Spanish movie theaters or on promenades; the husks rained to the floor. A group of boys with sports bags kept bringing new cassettes to the driver, who willingly broadcast their music over the loudspeakers mounted above every pair of seats, instead of the afternoon radio program. The one elderly couple on the bus sat silent and motionless. The husband seemed not to notice when one of the boys unintentionally jostled him every time he went up front; he put up with it even when one of the young fellows stood up while talking and stepped into the aisle, leaned on the back of the old man's seat, and gesticulated right in his face. He did not stir, did not even shift his newspaper to one side when the edges of the pages curled in the breeze created by the boy's gestures. The girl got off the bus and set out alone over a bleak knoll, her coat drawn close around her as she headed across a seemingly trackless steppe without a house in sight; on the floor beneath her vacated seat lay a heap of husks, not as big as one would have expected.

Later the plateau was punctuated by sparse oak groves, the trees small like shrubs, the withered leaves trembling grayish in the branches, and, after an almost unnoticeable pass—in Spanish the word was the same as for harbor, as the traveler learned from his pocket dictionary—which formed the border between the provinces of Burgos and Soria, came plantations of gleaming brown pines rooted atop cliffs, many of the trees also torn from their bit of soil and split, as after a storm, whereupon this closeness on either side of the road immediately gave way again to the prevailing barren landscape. At intervals the road was crossed by the rusted tracks of the abandoned rail line between the two cities, in many places tarred over, the ties overgrown or completely invisible. In one of the villages, out of sight of the road beyond rocky outcroppings—which the bus turned onto and from which, now even emptier, it had to return to the road—a loose street sign banged against the wall of a house; through the window of the village bar, the only thing visible, the hands of cardplayers.

In Soria it was cold, even colder than in Burgos, and bitter cold in comparison to San Sebastián down there by the sea, where he had come into Spain the previous day. But the snow he had been hoping for as a sort of companion to his undertaking did not fall; there was drizzle instead. In the drafty bus station he immediately noted down the times of departure for Madrid, or at least Zaragoza. Outside, on the main road at the edge of the town, between smaller tumbledown houses, shells of high-rises, and the rock-strewn steppe (which otherwise appealed to him), tractor-trailer trucks that seemed coupled together, all with Spanish license plates, thundered past, their wheels splattering a film of mud. When he caught sight of an English marker among them, and then the slogan on the canvas cover that he could understand at a glance, without having to translate it first, he felt for a moment almost at home. Similarly, during a longish stay in just such a foreign Spanish town, where no one knew any other language and there were no foreign newspapers, he had sometimes taken refuge in the only Chinese restaurant, where he actually understood even less of the language but felt safe from all that concentrated Spanish.

It was beginning to get dark, and outlines were blurring. The only highway signs pointed to distant capitals such as Barcelona and Valladolid. So he set out down the street with his heavy suitcase—he had been traveling a long time and had intended to stay in Soria into the New Year. He had found several times that the centers of these Spanish towns, which at first glance seemed almost invisible, were somewhere down below, beyond steppe-like stretches without houses, hidden in the valleys of dried-up rivers. He would stay here at least for the night; this once—he actually felt it as a sort of obligation—he had to get to know the place, now that he was here, and also do it justice (although at the moment, shifting his suitcase from one hand to the other every few steps and trying to avoid bumping into the natives, just beginning their evening ritual of strutting along, straight ahead, he did not succeed), and besides, as far as his "Essay on the Jukebox" was concerned, and in general, he had time, as he told himself now, as often before, in this instance using a verb from the Greek, borrowed from his reading of Theophrastus: *s-cholazo, s-cholazo.*

Yet all he could think of was running away. For his project, one friend or another had offered him, who for some years now had been roaming about without a home, his second apartment or third house, standing empty as winter came on, with silence all around, at the same time in a familiar culture, above all with the language of his childhood, which stimulated (and at the same time soothed) him right there on the horizon, to be reached at any time on foot. Yet his thought of running away did not include going back to where he came from. German-speaking surroundings were out of the question for him now, as was, for example, La Rochelle, with French, which was like second nature to him, where a few days ago he had felt like a stranger in the face of the wide Atlantic, the squat, pastel houses, the many movie theaters, the depopulated side streets, the clock tower by the old harbor that reminded him of Georges Simenon and those of his books that were set there. Not even San Sebastián with its much warmer air and clearly visible semicircular bay on the often turbulent Bay of Biscay, where just a short while ago, before his eyes, the floodwaters had surged upstream at night along the banks of the Basque Urumea River—while in the middle the current had flowed toward the sea—and in a bar, unlit and cold, as if it had been out of operation for years, stood a jukebox, made in Spain, clumsy, almost without design. Perhaps it was a compulsion in him that he forbade himself to run away, to retrace any of his steps, permitting himself only to move on, ever onward across the continent—and perhaps also a compulsion that now that he found himself without obligations and commitments, after a period of being much in demand, he felt that to get started on writing he had to subject himself, if writing was to have any justification at all, to barely tolerable, inhospitable conditions, to a marginal situation that threatened the very basis of daily life, with the added factor that, along with the project of writing, a second project had to be essayed: a sort of investigation or sounding out of each foreign place, and exposure of himself, alone, without benefit of teachers, to a language that at first had to be as unfamiliar as possible.

· · ·

Yet now he wanted to run away, not only from this town but also from his topic. The closer he had come to Soria, the intended site for writing, the more insignificant his subject, the "jukebox," had appeared. The year 1989 was just coming to an end, a year in which in Europe, from day to day and from country to country, so many things seemed to be changing, and with such miraculous ease, that he imagined that someone who had gone for a while without hearing the news, for instance voluntarily shut up in a research station or having spent months in a coma after an accident, would, upon reading his first newspaper, think it was a special joke edition pretending that the wish dreams of the subjugated and separated peoples of the continent had overnight become reality. This year, even for him, who had a background devoid of history and a childhood and youth scarcely enlivened, at most hindered, by historic events (and their neck-craning cele- brations), was the year of history: suddenly it seemed as if history, in addition to all its other forms, could be a self-narrating fairy tale, the most real and realistic, the most heavenly and earthly of fairy tales. A few weeks earlier, in Germany, an acquaintance, about to set out to see the Wall, now suddenly open, where he was "deter- mined to be a witness to history," had urged him to come along so that these events could be "witnessed by a person good with imagery and language." And he? He had used the excuse of "work, gathering material, preparations"— immediately, instinctively, actually shrinking from the experience, without thinking (though picturing how the very next morning the leading national newspaper would carry, properly framed, the first batch of poems produced by the poetic witnesses to history, and the following morning, likewise, the first song lyrics). And now that history was apparently moving along, day after day, in the guise of the great fairy tale of the world, of humanity, weaving its magic (or was it merely a variation on the old ghost story?), he wanted to be here, far away, in this city surrounded by steppes and bleak cliffs and deaf to history, where, in front of the televisions that blared everywhere, all the people fell silent only once, during a local news item about a man killed by collapsing scaffolding—and here he wanted to essay the unworldly topic of the jukebox, suitable for "refugees from the world," as he told himself now; a mere plaything, according to the literature, to be sure, "the Americans' favorite," but only for the short span of that "Saturday-night fever" after the end of the war. Was there anyone in the present time, when every day was a new historic date, more ridiculous, more perverse than himself?

He did not really take this thought seriously. Of far greater concern was the realization that his little project seemed to contradict what was occurring, more and more powerfully and urgently with the passing years, in the deepest of his nocturnal dreams. There, in the dream depths, his inner pattern revealed itself to him as an image, as image upon image: this he experienced with great force in his sleep, and he continued to dwell on it after awakening. Those dreams insistently told him a story; they told, though only in monumental fragments, which often degenerated into the usual dream nonsense, a world-encompassing epic of war and peace, heaven and earth, West and East, bloody murder, oppression, rebellion and reconciliation, castles and hovels, jungles and sports arenas, going astray and coming home, triumphal unions between total strangers and sacramental marital love, with innumerable, sharply delineated characters: familiar strangers, neighbors who came and went over the decades, distant siblings, film stars and politicians, saints and sinners, ancestors who lived on in these dreams transformed (as they had been in reality), and always new to the children, to the child of the children, who was one of the main characters.

As a rule he himself did not appear, was merely a spectator and listener. As forceful as the images were the feelings this person had; some of them he never experienced while awake, for instance reverence for a simple human face, or ecstasy at the dream blue of a mountain, or even piety (this, too, a feeling) in the face of nothing but the realization "I'm here"; he was acquainted with other feelings as well, but they did not become pure and incarnate to him except in the sensuous intensity of his epic dreaming, where he now experienced not gratitude but the very essence of gratitude, likewise the essence of compassion, the essence of childlikeness, the essence of hatred, the essence of amazement, the essence of friendship, of grief, of abandonment, of fear in the face of death.

. . .

Awakening, as if aired out and leavened by such dreams, he felt spreading in waves far beyond him the rhythm he would have to follow with his writing. And again, not for the first time, he was postponing this task, in favor of something inconsequential? (It was those dreams that engendered such thoughts; no one else had authority over him.) And his habit of thinking that, transient as he was, he could commit himself only to occasional pieces— after all, Simenon's short novels, most of them written abroad, in hotel rooms, could hardly be said to have epic breadth—wasn't that again, as his dream reproached him, one of those excuses he had been using for too long now? Why didn't he settle down, no matter where? Didn't he notice that his travels were more and more just a kind of aimless wandering?

When the "Essay on the Jukebox" had been merely a glimmer, he had had in mind as a possible motto something Picasso had said: One made pictures the way princes made their children—with shepherdesses. One never portrayed the Pantheon, one never painted a Louis XV fauteuil, but one made pictures with a cottage in the Midi, with a packet of tobacco, with an old chair. But the closer he came to carrying out his plan, the less applicable this painter's saying seemed to a writer's subject matter. The epic dreams manifested themselves too powerfully, too exclusively, and also too contagiously (infecting him with a yearning to translate them into the appropriate language). He was familiar with the phenomenon from his youth, yet always amazed at how, toward the winter solstice, night after night these dreams turned up, predictably, so to speak; with the first image of half sleep the gate to narrative swung open, and narrative chanted to him all night long. And besides: what did an object like the jukebox, made of plastic, colored glass, and chromed metal, have to do with a chair or a cottage? — Nothing. — Or perhaps something, after all?

He knew of no painter in whose work there was a jukebox, even as an accessory. Not even the Pop artists, with their magnifying view of everything mass-produced, non-original, derivative, seemed to find the jukebox worth bringing into focus. Standing in front of a few paintings by Edward Hopper, with isolated figures in the dim bars of an urban no-man's-land, he almost had a hallucination, as if the objects were there, but painted over, as it were, an empty, glowing spot. Only one singer came to mind, Van Morrison, to whom the "roar of the jukebox" had remained significant forever, but that was "long gone," a folk expression for "long ago."

And besides: why did his picture of what there was to say of this object immediately take the form of a book, even if only a very small one? After all, wasn't this thing called a book intended, as he conceived it, for the reflection, sentence by sentence, of natural light, of the sun, above all, but not for the description of the dimming artificial light produced by the revolving cylinders of an electrical device. (At least this was the traditional image of a book that he could not shake off.) So wasn't a small piece of writing like this more suitable for a newspaper, preferably for the weekend magazine, on the nostalgia pages, with color photographs of jukebox models from the earliest times to the present?

Having reached this point in his ruminations, ready simply to drop everything toward which his thoughts had pointed in recent months ("Be silent about what is dear to you, and write about what angers and provokes you!"), resolved to enjoy his time for a while, doing nothing and continuing to be a sightseer on the Continent, he suddenly experienced a remarkable pleasure in the possible meaninglessness of his project—freedom!—and at the same time the energy to get to work on this little nothing, though if possible somewhere other than in this world-forsaken town of Soria.

For the night he found a room in a hotel named after a medieval Spanish king. Almost every strange place he had encountered on his travels that had seemed at first sight insignificant and isolated had revealed itself to him, when he set out to walk it, as unexpectedly spread out, as part of the world; "What a big city!" he had marveled again and again, and even "What a big town!" But Soria, to whose narrow streets he entrusted himself on that rainy evening, did not expand, even when he groped his way in the dark out of town and uphill to where the ruined citadel stood; no glittering *avenida*; the town, nothing but a few faded boxlike walls at the bend in the narrow streets, revealed itself to him, as he then wandered from bar to bar, all of them almost empty already, enlivened now by the repetitious siren songs of the slot machines, as an all-too-familiar Central European town, only with more blackness within the city limits—the winter-deserted oval of the bullfighting ring—and surrounded by blackness. He had already concluded that nothing remained to be discovered and generated there. But for now it was nice to be walking without luggage. The front row of a book-store's display consisted exclusively of books by Harold Robbins—and why not? And in a small square toward midnight the damp, jagged leaves of the plane trees glittered and beckoned. And the ticket booths of the two movie houses, the Rex and the Avenida, had their windows, almost invisible, as only in Spain, next to the wide entrances, looking directly out on the street, and inside, half cut off by the frames, showed the face of what seemed the identical old woman. And the wine did not have a small-town taste. And the pattern on the sidewalk tiles in the town of Soria consisted of interlocking squares, rounded at the edges, while the corresponding pattern in the city of Burgos had been battlements? And the Spanish word for equanimity was *ecuanimidad*. He made up a litany with this word, alternating it with that Greek word for having time.

In his dream, a hundred people appeared. A general, at the same time an epigone of Shakespeare, shot himself out of sorrow at the state of the world. A hare fled across a field, a duck swam downriver. A child disappeared without a trace, before everyone's eyes. The villagers, according to hearsay, were dying from one hour to the next, and the priest was completely taken up with burials. (Strange, the role of hearsay in dreams—it was neither said nor heard, but simply moved silently through the air.) Grandfather's nosebleeds smelled of damp dog hair. Another child had the first name "Soul." Someone proclaimed, loudly this time, the importance of hearing in these times.

The next day—it remained rainy, and according to the newspaper, Soria was again the coldest province in Spain—he set out for a farewell stroll through town. Without having intended it, he suddenly found himself standing before the façade of Santo Domingo, its age immediately revealed by its dimensions and the light sandstone, worn smooth in many places by the wind. What a jolt he always received from Romanesque structures; he at once felt their proportions in himself, in his shoulders, his hips, the soles of his feet, like his actual, hidden body. Yes, corporeality: that was the sensation with which he now approached, as slowly as possible, this church shaped like a grain box, in a wide arc. In the very first moment, taking in the delicacy of the surface with its rounded arches and figures, he had thought of a phrase used by Borges, "the brotherliness of the beautiful," yet at the same time he was overcome with reluctance to absorb the whole thing at once, and he decided to postpone until evening departing for who knows where, and before leaving to come back again, when the daylight on the stone carvings would have changed. For the time being, he merely tried to identify variations in the groups of figures, already dear and familiar to him. And variations there were (without his having to look for them very long), as always in Romanesque sculpture, and they appeared to him again as the secret emblems of the place. Here in Soria they were visible as far as the eye could see: the solicitous way God the Father bent at the hips as he helped the newly created Adam to his feet; the blanket, almost smooth in one representation, in other portrayals consistently lumpy, under which the Three Kings slumbered; the acanthus leaf, shell-shaped, the size of a tree, that rose behind the empty tomb after the Resurrection; in a semicircle above the portal (in almond form the outline of the smiling father with the likewise smiling son on his knees, balancing the thick stone book), the allegorical animals representing the Evangelists, crouching not on the ground but on the laps of angels, and not just the apparently newborn lion cub and the bull calf, but even the mighty eagle . . .

As he hurried away, he looked back over his shoulder and saw the delicately carved housing—all the more clearly its emptiness—standing, in the expression used by the cabaret artist Karl Valentin, "out in the open": from this vantage point, the structure, as broad as it was squat (all the apartment buildings around it were taller), with the sky above, in spite of the trucks roaring by, offered a positively ideal image: the building, so utterly different from the rigid façades surrounding it, appeared playful, active precisely in its tranquillity—it was playing. And the thought came to him that back then, eight hundred years ago, at least in Europe, for the duration of one stylistic period, human history, individual as well as collective, had been wonderfully clear. Or was that only the illusion conveyed by this absolutely consistent form (not a mere style)? But how had such a form, at once majestic and childlike, and so readily comprehended, emerged?

Soria, as became apparent now by day, lay between two hills, one wooded and one bare, in a valley sloping down to the Duero. The river flowed past the last, scattered houses, on the other side a vast expanse of craggy land. A stone bridge spanned the river, bearing the road to Zaragoza. At the same time as the arches, the newly arrived observer noted their number. A gentle wind was blowing, and the clouds were in motion. Down there, among the leafless poplars along the bank, an excited dog was chasing the leaves that swirled up now here, now there. The reeds were flattened into the dark water; only a few cattails stuck out. The stranger—strange?—given access here by the locale—struck out in the opposite direction toward the well-known promenade of the poet Machado and went upriver, following a dirt path crisscrossed by the roots of the pines. Silence; a current of air at his temples (he had once imagined that one of the manufacturers responsible for such things might offer for these parts of the face a special moisturizer, so that even the slightest puff of air would be felt by the skin, as the epitome of—what should one call it?—the here-and-now).

Back from the wide-open spaces, he had a cup of coffee in a bar down by the river called Río, a young gypsy behind the counter. A few retired men—the Spanish word, according to the dictionary, was *jubilados*—were without exception watching the morning TV program with utter concentration and enthusiasm. From the incessant traffic passing on the highway, glasses and cups shook in the hands of all those present. In one corner stood a barely knee-high cylindrical cast-iron stove, tapered toward the top, with vertical fluting and in the middle an ornament like a scallop shell; in the grate down below the fire glowed red-hot. From the tiled floor rose the scent of the fresh sawdust that had been strewn that morning.

Out on the street, as he was climbing the hill, he came upon an elder, its trunk as thick as a sequoia, its short, bright branches forming a myriad of interwoven and crisscrossed arches. No superstition, even without such signs and portents: he would stay in Soria and, as planned, get to work on his "essay." In between he intended to soak up as much as possible of the mornings and evenings of this easily read little city. "No, I'm not leaving until the thing is done!" In Soria he would watch the last leaves sail off the plane trees. And now the landscape was bathed in that dark, clear light, as if streaming from the earth below, that had always encouraged him to go off at once and write, write, write—without a subject, or for that matter on something like the jukebox. And out into the wide-open spaces, with which here, scarcely out of town, one was promptly surrounded—in which major cities was that the case?—was where he would go every day before sitting down to work, to find the peace and quiet his head required more and more as he got older; once tuned to the silence, the sentences were supposed to take shape on their own; but afterwards he would expose himself to the racket, as well as the quieter corners, of the city; no passageway, no cemetery, no bar, no playing field could be left unnoticed in its respective uniqueness.

But it turned out that just now several Spanish holidays fell at the same time—travel time—and so there would be no rooms available in Soria until the beginning of the following week. That was all right with him; it meant he could again postpone getting started, his usual pattern. And besides, forced to decamp temporarily to another city, he could, upon his departure and return, form a picture of Soria's location, remote on the high plateau, also from other directions, not only the westerly one from Burgos; he imagined that would be useful for what lay ahead. So he had two days, and he decided to spend the first in the north, the second in the south, both in places that lay outside Castile, first Logroño in the wine-growing region of La Rioja, then in Zaragoza in Aragon; this plan emerged mainly from his study of the bus schedules. But for the time being he sat down in one of those Spanish

back-room restaurants where he felt sheltered because
there one could be by oneself and yet, through walls no
thicker than planks and the frequently open sliding door,
follow what was going on out in the bar, where, what
with a television set and pinball machines, things were
almost always pretty lively.

In mid-afternoon a nun was the only other passenger on
the bus to Logroño. It was raining, and in the mountain
pass between the two provinces the route seemed to lead
through the middle of the main rain cloud; other than
its billowing grayness, there was nothing to be seen
through the windows. From the bus's radio came "Sat-
isfaction" by the Rolling Stones, a song that more than
any other stood for that "roar of the jukebox," and was
one of very few that had held their own in jukeboxes all
over the world (had not been replaced), a "classic," one
of the passengers thought to himself—while the other, in
her black monastic garb, talked with the driver, to the
accompaniment of the space-filling sonority of Bill Wy-
man's guitar, which seemed to command respect, about
the construction accident that had occurred in a side street
nearby while he was eating in his sheltered back-room
restaurant: two men crushed under reinforcing rods and
freshly poured concrete. Next came Jacques Brel's "Ne
me quitte pas" on the radio, that song pleading with the
beloved not to leave him, another of those few songs that
constituted what might be called the classics of the jukebox, at least according to his inquiries in French-speaking
countries, and listed as a rule on the far right in the

sacrosanct column (where in Austrian music boxes, for example, one found so-called folk music, and in Italian ones operatic arias and choruses, above all "Celeste Aïda" and the prisoners' chorus from *Nabucco*). But it was strange, the traveler thought, that the Belgian singer's psalm, rising out of the depths, the human voice almost alone, holding nothing back, searingly personal—"I tell you this, and you alone!"—did not seem at all suitable for an automatic record player set up in a public place, coin-operated, yet did seem suitable here, in this almost empty bus taking the curves of a pass almost two thousand meters above sea level, crossing a gray no-man's-land of dreary drizzle and fog.

The pattern of the sidewalk tiles in Logroño was bunches of grapes and grape leaves, and the town had an official chronicler with a daily page to himself in the newspaper, *La Rioja*. Instead of the Duero, the river here was the headwaters of the Ebro, and instead of being on the edge of town, it ran straight through the middle, with the newer part of the city as usual on the opposite bank. High snowbanks lined the wide river; on closer inspection, they turned out to be industrial effluent rocking in the current, and against the façades of the tall buildings on both sides of the river, laundry flapped in the dusky rain. Although he had observed a similar sight in Soria, and although Logroño, down here in the wine-growing plains with a noticeably milder climate, showed itself in its holiday illumination to be an expansive, elegant city with *avenidas* and arcades, he felt something like the tug of homesickness at the prospect of settling in for the winter up there on the *meseta*, where he had spent barely a night and half a day.

Zaragoza on the following day, to the southeast and even farther down in the broad Ebro Valley, had its sidewalks decorated with looping serpentines, which, he thought, represented the meanders of the river, and in fact the town appeared to him, after his first fruitless wanderings in search of the center, a pattern by now familiar to him in Spain, as a royal city, as indicated by the name of the soccer club. Here he could have read foreign newspapers every day, seen all the latest films in the original language, as only in a metropolis, and been there on the weekends when one royal team played against another from Madrid, with Emilio Butragueño himself on the ball—he had a pair of small binoculars in his luggage. Butragueño's uniform was always clean, even in the mud, and one felt one could believe him when he once replied to a reporter who asked whether soccer was an art form: "Yes, for seconds at a time." In the city's theater Beckett was being performed, and people were buying tickets as they did at movie box offices, and in the art museum, looking at the paintings of Goya, who had served his apprenticeship here in Zaragoza, he could have acquired the same receptivity of the senses for work as out there in the stillness around Soria, as well as the agreeable impertinence with which this painter infected one. Yet now only the other town could be considered, where, on the rock-strewn slopes adjacent to the new construction, flocks of sheep had

71

already worn paths and where, despite the altitude, sparrows flew straight up in the wind—he would have missed them. (Someone had once observed that something you could always count on seeing on the television news, in an on-location report, whether from Tokyo or Johannesburg, was the sparrows: in the foreground a group of statesmen lined up for the camera, or smoking ruins; in the background the sparrows.)

What he undertook to do instead in these two cities was to look casually for a jukebox; there had to be at least one in Logroño as in Zaragoza, from earlier times and still in operation (a newly installed one was unlikely; in the Spanish bars the least bit of free space belonged to the slot machines that were squeezed in, one on top of the other). He thought that in the course of time he had developed a sort of instinct for possible jukebox locations. There was little hope downtown, or in urban renewal areas, or near historic monuments, churches, parks, avenues (not to mention the fancy residential sections). He had almost never come upon a music box in a spa or winter resort (although the usually unknown, out-of-the-way neighboring communities were under suspicion, so to speak—O Samedan near Saint Moritz), almost never in yacht harbors or seaside resorts (but certainly in fishing harbors and, even more frequently, in ferry stations: O Dover, O Ostende, O Reggio di Calabria, O Piraeus, O Kyle of Lochalsh with the ferry across to the Inner Hebrides, O Aomori far in the north of the Japanese main island of Hondo, with the meanwhile discontinued ferry over to Hokkaido), less frequently in bars on the mainland and in the interior than on islands and near borders. In his experience, the following locations were especially hot: housing developments along highways, too sprawling to be villages, yet without a downtown, off the beaten track for any kind of tourist traffic, in almost uncontoured plains without lakes nearby (and if there was a river, far outside of town and dried up during most of the year), inhabited by unusual numbers of foreigners, foreign workers and/or soldiers (garrisons), and even there jukeboxes could be ferreted out neither in the middle— this often marked by nothing more than a larger rain puddle—nor on the outskirts (there, or even farther out, along the highways, one found at most a discotheque), but in between, most likely next to the barracks, by the railroad station, in the gas-station bar, or in an isolated saloon along a canal (of course in a bad neighborhood, "on the other side of the freight tracks," for instance, the face of the most faceless conglomerations). Such a prime location for a jukebox, aside from the one of his birth, he had once found on the Friuli plain, in Casarza, which has given itself the epithet "della Delizia" because of the type of grapes harvested in the region. From the pleasant, wealthy, jukebox-purged capital of Udine he had arrived there one summer evening, "behind the Tagliamento," going on only six words from a poem by Pasolini, who had spent part of his youth in this small town and later had castigated the jukeboxes of Rome, together with the pinball machines, as an American continuation of the war by other means: "in the desperate void of Casarza." After an attempted walking tour that would include the outskirts of town, soon broken off because of the traffic on all the arterial roads, he turned around, went at random into the bars, of which there were not a few, and in almost every one he could see from the entrance a jukebox glowing at him (one fancy one had a VCR with a screen above it, from which the sound also emanated). And all these variously shaped old and new boxes were in operation, playing not background music, as was often the case elsewhere, but loud, insistent music; they were blaring. It was a Sunday evening, and in the bars—the closer he got to the railroad station, the more so—farewells were taking place or recruits were already waiting out the last hours before having to report for duty at midnight, most of them apparently having just returned by train from a short furlough. As it got later, most of them no longer formed groups but sat there by themselves. They gathered around a Wurlitzer, a reproduction of the classic rainbow-shaped type, with bubbles pulsing around the rainbow. The soldiers were clustered so thickly that the blinking lights of the machine peeked through their bodies here and there, and their faces and necks, bent toward the record arm, were bathed alternately in blue, red, and yellow. The street across from the station formed a wide curve behind them and immediately disappeared into the darkness. In the station bar itself, the surfaces were already being washed down. But a couple of the fellows in gray-and-brown uniforms were still hovering near the jukebox, some of them with their duffel bags already on their shoulders. Here, to match the neon lighting, the jukebox

was a newer, no-nonsense model in bright metal. Each
man stood there by himself, and at the same time as if
in formation around the apparatus, which, in the otherwise empty room, with the tables shoved against the wall
and a chair here and there, boomed out at a higher volume
over the damp tiled floor. While one of the soldiers
stepped aside as the mop approached, his eyes, wide open,
unblinking, remained fixed in one direction; another lin-
gered, his head turned back over his shoulder, on the
threshold. It was full moon, in the glass door the shaking,
rattling, pounding, long-drawn-out, of a dark freight
passing, which blocked the corn fields beyond the tracks.
At the bar the young woman with even, fine features and
a gap between her teeth.

But in these Spanish towns his instinct betrayed him every
time. Even in bars in the poorer parts of town, behind
piles of debris, at the end of a cul-de-sac, with that dim
lighting that here and there made him hasten his steps
even at a distance, he did not find so much as the coldest
trail, even in the form of a paler outline on a sooty wall,
of the object he sought. The music played there came—
standing outside, he sometimes let himself be deceived
through the walls—from radios, cassette players, or, in
special cases, from a record player. The Spanish street
bars, and there seemed to be more of them in every town
than anywhere else in the world, were perhaps either too
new for such an almost ancient object (and all lacked the
back rooms suitable for it), or too old, and intended mainly
for old people, who sat there seriously playing cards—

jukebox and cardplaying, yes, but only in the less serious establishments—or sat with their heads propped in their hands, alone. And he imagined that in their heyday juke-boxes had been banned by the dictatorship here, and after that had simply not been in demand. To be sure, he made not a few discoveries in the course of his futile searching, taking a certain pleasure in the almost sure fruitlessness of it, about the special corners, the variations in the seem-ingly so similar cities.

Back from Zaragoza in Soria, of whose eastern province he had seen hardly anything, traveling at night on a rail-road line that ran far from any roads, he now needed a room suitable for his essay; he wanted to get started—finally—the very next day. Up high on one of the two hills, or down below in the midst of the town? Up high, and by definition outside of town, he would perhaps feel too cut off again, and surrounded by streets and houses too confined. A room looking out on an inner courtyard made him too melancholy, one looking out on a square distracted him too much, one facing north would have too little sun for writing, in one facing south the paper would blind him when the sun was shining, on the bare hill the wind would blow in, on the wooded one dogs being walked would be barking all day, in the pensions —he checked out all of them—the other guests would be too near, in the hotels, which he also circled, he would probably be alone too much in winter for a good writing mood. For the night he took a room in the hotel on the bare hill. The street leading up to it ended in front of the stone building in a muddy square; the footpath into town—he tried it out at once—led through a steppe covered with moss and thistles, then past the façade of Santo Domingo, its very existence stimulating when he looked at it, and straight to the small squares, whose dimensions included plane trees, evocative of the mountains, the remaining leaves swaying in the breeze, curiously full at the tips of the highest branches, glittering star-shaped against the night-black sky. The room up there appealed to him also: not too confining and not too spacious—as a rule, he did not feel as if he was in the right place when there was too much space. The city, not too close and not too far, also not too far below, shone into the neither too large-paned nor too small-paned window, toward which he shoved the table, away from the mirror, experimenting further: a tiny table, to be sure, but enough of a surface for a piece of paper, pencils, and an eraser. He felt well taken care of here; this was his place for the time being.

When the next morning came, he experimented with sitting at the right hour, testing the light as it would really be, the temperature as it should be for the essay: now the room was too noisy for him (yet he should have known that precisely in so-called quiet locations the noises posed far more of a risk to collecting one's thoughts than on the loudest streets, for they came abruptly instead of steadily—suddenly the radio, laughter, echoes, a chair scraping, something popping, hissing, and, to make it worse, from close by and inside the building, from corridors, neighboring rooms, the ceiling; once the writer's concentration was lost, the image got away from him, and without that, no language). Then it was strange that the next room was not only too cold for sitting hour after hour (didn't he know that only luxury hotels kept the heat on during the day, and that, besides, when the writing was going well, he involuntarily always breathed in such a way that he didn't feel the cold?), but this time also too quiet, as if the enclosed spaces meant being locked in and a sense of openness were available only outdoors in nature, and how to let this kind of quiet in the window in December?

The third room had two beds—one too many for him. The fourth room had only one door separating it from the next room—at least one too few for him . . . In this way he learned the Spanish word for "too much," a very long word, *demasiado*. Wasn't one of Theophrastus' "characters" or types that man "dissatisfied with the given," who, upon being kissed by his sweetheart, says he wonders whether she also loves him with her soul, and who is angry with Zeus, not because he makes it rain but because the rain comes too late, and who, finding a money purse on the path, says, "But I've never found a treasure!"? And a child's rhyme also came to mind, about someone who was never happy anywhere, and he changed the words a little: "A little man I knew was puzzled what to do. / At home it was too cold, so he went into the wood. / In the wood it was too moist—soft grass was his next choice. / Finding the grass too green, he went next

---

to Berlin. / Berlin was far too large, so he bought himself
a barge. / The barge proved far too small, so he went
home after all. / At home . . ." Wasn't this the recognition
that he wasn't in the right place anywhere? On the contrary, he had always been in the right place somewhere
—for instance?—in locations where he had got down to
writing—or where a jukebox stood (though not in private
dwellings!). So he had been in the right place wherever,
in any case and from the outset, it was clear that in the
long run he couldn't stay?

Finally he took the room that turned up next, and it was
good; whatever challenges came his way—he would ac-
cept them. "Who will win out—the noise or us?" He
sharpened his bundle of pencils out the window, pencils
he had bought in all different countries during his years
of traveling, and then again often German brands: how
small one of them had become since that January in
Edinburgh—was it already that long ago? As the pencil
curls swirled away in the wind, they mixed with ash from
the smoke of a wood fire, as down below, in front of the
building, by the kitchen door, which gave directly on the
thistle-, rock-, and moss-steppe, an apprentice with a knife
as long as his arm was cleaning a pile of even longer fish,
the gleaming scales of the fish shooting sparkling into the
air. "A good sign or not?" — But now, after all this, it
was too late in the day to get started. Accustomed to
postponing his form of play, he felt once again actually
relieved and used the delay for a walk out onto the steppe,
in order to check out a few possible paths for the quality

of their soil—not too hard, not too soft—and for the atmospheric conditions: not too exposed to westerly storms, but also not too sheltered.

Meanwhile something was happening to him. When he first had the inspiration—that's what it was—which at once made sense to him—of writing an "essay on the jukebox," he had pictured it as a dialogue onstage: this object, and what it could mean to an individual, was for most people so bizarre that an idea presented itself: having one person, a sort of audience representative, assume the role of interrogator, and a second appear as an "expert" on the subject, in contrast to Platonic dialogues, where the one who asked the questions, Socrates, secretly knew more about the problem than the other, who, puffed up with preconceptions, at least at the beginning, claimed to know the answer; perhaps it would be most effective if the expert, too, discovered only when he had to field the other's questions what the relative "place value" of these props had been in the drama of his life. In the course of time the stage dialogue faded from his mind, and the "essay" hovered before him as an unconnected composite of many different forms of writing, corresponding to the—what should he call it—uneven? arrhythmic? ways in which he had experienced a jukebox and remembered it: momentary images should alternate with blow-by-blow narratives, suddenly broken off; mere jottings would be followed by a detailed reportage about a single music box, together with a specific locale; from a pad of notes would come, without transition, a leap to one with quotations, which, again without transition, without harmonizing linkage, would make way perhaps to a litany-like recitation of the titles and singers listed on a particular find —he pictured, as the underlying form that would give the whole thing a sort of coherence, the question-and-answer play recurring periodically, though in fragmentary fashion, and receding again, joined by similarly fragmentary filmed scenes, each organized around a different jukebox, from which would emanate all sorts of happenings or a still life, in ever widening circles—which could extend as far as a different country, or only to the beech at the end of a railroad platform. He hoped he could have his "essay" fade out with a "Ballad of the Jukebox," a singable, so to speak "rounded" song about this thing, though only if, after all the leaps in imagery, it emerged on its own.

It had seemed to him that such a writing process was appropriate not merely to the particular subject matter but also to the times themselves. Didn't the narrative forms of previous eras—their consistency, their gestures of conjuring up and mastering (strangers' destinies), their claim to totality, as amateurish as it was naïve—when employed in modern books strike him nowadays as mere bluster? Varied approximations, some minor, some major, and in permeable forms, instead of the standard imprisoning forms, were what he felt books should be now, precisely because of his most complete, intense, unifying experiences with objects: preserving distance; circumscribing; sketching in; flirting around—giving your subject a protective escort from the sidelines. And now, as he aimlessly checked out trails in the savanna, suddenly an entirely new rhythm sprang up in him, not an alternating, sporadic one, but a single, steady one, and, above all, one that, instead of circling and flirting around, went straight and with complete seriousness in medias res: the rhythm of narrative. At first he experienced everything he encountered as he went along as a component of the narrative; whatever he took in was promptly narrated inside him; moments in the present took place in the narrative past, and not as in dreams but, without any fuss, as mere assertions, short and sweet as the moment itself: "Thistles had blown into the wire fence. An older man with a plastic bag bent down for a mushroom. A dog hopped by on three legs and made one think of a deer; its coat was yellow, its face white; gray-blue smoke wafted over the scene from a stone cottage. The seedpods rustling in the only tree standing sounded like matchboxes being shaken. From the Duero leaped fish, the wind-blown waves upstream had caps of foam, and on the other bank the water lapped the foot of the cliffs. In the train from Zaragoza the lights were already lit, and a handful of people sat in the carriages . . ."

But then this quiet narration of the present also carried over into his impending "essay," conceived as varied and playful; it became transformed, even before the first sentence was written, into a narrative so compelling and powerful that all other forms promptly faded to insignificance. That did not seem terrible to him, but overwhelmingly splendid; for in the rhythm of this narration he heard the voice of warmth-giving imagination, in which he had continued to believe, though it all too seldom touched his inner heart: he believed in it precisely because of the stillness it brought, even in the midst of deafening racket; the stillness of nature, however far outside, was then nothing by comparison. And the characteristic feature of imagination was that in conjunction with its images the place and the locale where he would write his narrative appeared. True, there had been times in the past when he had felt a similar urge, but at such times he had relocated a birch in Cologne to Indianapolis as a cypress, or a cow path in Salzburg to Yugoslavia, or the place where he was writing had been consigned to the background as something unimportant; but this time Soria was to appear as Soria (perhaps also with Burgos, and also with Vitoria, where an old native had greeted him before he said anything), and would be as much the subject matter of the narrative as the jukebox.

Until far into the night he continued his observations in narrative form, though by now it had become a form of torture—literally every petty detail (the passerby with a toothpick in his mouth, the name Benita Soria Verde on a gravestone, the poet's elm, weighted with stones and concrete in honor of Antonio Machado, the missing letters in the HOTEL sign) imposed itself on him and wanted to be narrated. This was no longer the compelling, warming power of imagery carrying him along, but clearly a cold compulsion, ascending from his heart to his head, a senseless, repeated hurling of himself against a gate long since closed, and he wondered whether narration, which had first seemed divine, hadn't been a snare and a delusion —an expression of his fear in the face of all the isolated, unconnected phenomena? An escape? The result of cowardice? — But was a man walking along with a toothpick between his lips, in the winter, on the *meseta* of Castile, his nodded response to a greeting, really so insignificant? — Be that as it might: he did not want to know in advance the first sentence with which he would begin on the morrow; in the past, whenever he had hammered out the first sentence, he had promptly found himself blocked when it came to the second. — On the other hand: away with all such patterns! — And so on . . .

The morning of the following day. The table at the window of the hotel room. Empty plastic bags blowing across the rock-strewn landscape, catching here and there on the thistles. On the horizon, an escarpment shaped like a ski jump, with a rain-bearing mushroom cloud over the approach ramp. Closing his eyes. Jamming a wad of paper into the cracks around the window through which the wind whistles its worst. Closing his eyes again. Pulling out the table drawer whose handle rattles as soon as he begins to write. Closing his eyes for the third time. Howls of distress. Opening the window: a small black dog right beneath it, hitched to the foundation, drenched with rain as only a dog can be drenched; its wails, which briefly fall silent now and then, accompanied by clouds of breath visibly puffed out into the steppe. *Aullar* was the Spanish word for "howl." Closing his eyes for the fourth time.

On the ride from Logroño to Zaragoza he had seen the stone cubes of the vintners' huts out in the winter-deserted vineyards of the Ebro Valley. In the region he came from, one could also see such huts along the paths that led through the grain fields, though built of wood, and the size of a plank shed. On the inside they also looked like a shed, with the light coming only through the chinks between the boards and the knotholes, clumps of grass on the floor, stinging nettles in the corners, growing luxuriantly between the harvest tools leaning there. And yet each of the huts on the few acres his grandfather tenant-farmed felt to him like a realm unto itself. As a rule, an elder grew nearby, its crown providing shade for this thing set out in the middle of the field, and its arching branches forcing their way into the interior of the hut. And there was just room enough for a small table and a bench, which could also be set outside by the elder. Wrapped in cloths to keep fresh and be protected from insects, the jug of cider and some cake for a snack. In the domain of these sheds he had felt more at home than ever in solidly built houses. (In such houses, a comparable sense of being in the right place had come over him at most when he glanced into a windowless storage room or stood on the threshold between inside and outside, where one was still safe indoors while snow and rain from outside blew lightly against one.) Yet he viewed the field huts less as refuges than as places of rest or peace. Later it was enough simply to glimpse in his region a light gray, weathered storage shed, blown crooked by the wind, off in the distance by a fallow field, in passing; he would feel his heart leap up and dash to it and be at home in the hut for a moment, along with the flies of summer, the wasps of autumn, and the coldness of rusting chains in winter.

The huts back home had been gone for a long time. Only the much larger barns, used exclusively for hay storage, still existed. But long ago, at a time when the huts were still there, the domestic or localized magic they held for him had been transferred to jukeboxes. Even as an adolescent, with his parents, he didn't go to the inn or to have a soda, but to the "Wurlitzer" ("Wurlitzer is Jukebox" was the advertising slogan), to listen to records. What he had described as his sense of having arrived and feeling sheltered, each time only fleetingly, in the realm of the field huts was literally true of the music boxes as well. Yet the external form of the various devices and even the selections they offered meant at first less than the particular sound emanating from them. This sound did not come from above, as from the radio that stood at home in the corner with the shrine, but from underground, and also, although the volume might be the same, instead of from the usual tinny box, from an inner space whose vibrations filled the room. It was as if it were not an automatic device but rather an additional instrument that imbued the music—though only a certain kind of music, as he realized in retrospect—with its underlying sound, comparable perhaps to the rattling of a train, when it suddenly becomes, as the train passes over an iron bridge, a primeval thunder. Much later, a child was standing one time by such a jukebox (it was playing Madonna's "Like a Prayer," his own selection), the child still so small that the entire force of the loudspeaker down below was directed at his body. The child was listening, all ears, all solemn, all absorbed, while his parents had already reached the door, were ready to leave, calling to the child again and again, in between smiling at his behavior, as if to apologize for their offspring to the other patrons, until the song had died away and the child, still solemn and reverent, walked past his father and mother onto the street. (Did this suggest that the obelisk-shaped jukeboxes' lack of success had less to do with their unusual appearance than with the fact that the music was directed upward, toward the ceiling?)

Unlike with the field huts, he was not satisfied to have the jukeboxes simply stand there; they had to be ready to play, quietly humming—even better than having just been set in motion by a stranger's hand—lit up as brightly as possible, as if from their inner depths; there was nothing more mournful than a dark, cold, obsolete metal box, possibly even shamefacedly hidden from view under a crocheted Alpine throw. Yet that did not quite correspond to the facts, for he now recalled a defective jukebox in the Japanese temple site of Nikko, the first one encountered in that country after a long journey between south and north, hidden under bundles of magazines, the coin slot covered over with a strip of tape and promptly uncovered by him—but at any rate there, at last. To celebrate this find he had drunk another saké and let the train to Tokyo out there in the darkness depart without him. Before that, at an abandoned temple site way up in the woods, he had passed a still smoldering peat fire, next to it a birch broom and a mound of snow, and farther along in the mountainous terrain a boulder had poked out of a brook, and as the water shot over it, it had sounded just like the water in a certain other rocky-mountain brook—as if one were receiving, if one's ears were open to it, the broadcast of a half-sung, half-drummed speech before the plenary session of the united nations of a planet far off in the universe. Then, at night in Tokyo, people had stepped over others lying every which way on the railroad steps, and even later, again in a temple precinct, a drunk had stopped before the incense burner, had prayed, and then staggered off into the darkness.

It was not only the belly resonance: the "American hits" had also sounded entirely different to him back then on the jukeboxes of his native land than on the radio in his house. He always wanted the radio volume turned up when Paul Anka sang his "Diana," Dion his "Sweet Little Sheila," and Ricky Nelson his "Gypsy Woman," but at the same time he felt guilty that such non-music appealed to him (later, when he was at the university and finally had a record player in his room, with the radio as an amplifier, for the first few years it was reserved for what was conventionally felt to deserve the name of music).

But from the jukebox he boldly unleashed the trills, howls, shouts, rattling, and booming that not merely gave him pleasure but filled him with shudders of rapture, warmth, and fellowship. In the reverberating steel-guitar ride of "Apache," the cold, stale, and belch-filled Espresso Bar on the highway from the "City of the Plebiscite of 1920" to the "City of the Popular Uprising of 1938" got plugged into an entirely different kind of electricity, with which one could choose, on the glowing scale at hip-level, numbers from "Memphis, Tennessee," felt oneself turning into the mysterious "handsome stranger," and heard the rumbling and squeaking of the trucks outside transformed into the steady roar of a convoy on "Route 66," with the thought: No matter where to—just out of here!

Although back home the music boxes had also been a gathering point for Saturday-night dances—a large semi-circle around them was usually left clear—he himself would never have thought of joining in. He did enjoy watching the dancers, who in the dimness of the cafés became mere outlines around the massive illuminated case whose rumble seemed to come out of the ground—but for him a jukebox, like the field huts earlier, was a source of peace, or something that made one feel peaceful, made one sit still, in relative motionlessness or breathlessness, interrupted only by the measured, positively ceremonial act of "going to push the buttons." And in listening to a jukebox he was never beside himself, or feverish, or dreamy, as he otherwise was with music that affected him—even strictly classical music, and the seemingly rapturous music of earlier, preceding eras. The dangerous part about listening to music, someone had once told him, was the propensity it had to make one perceive something that remained to be done as already done. The jukebox sound of his early years, on the other hand, literally caused him to collect himself, and awakened, or activated, his images of what might be possible and encouraged him to contemplate them.

The places where one could mull things over as nowhere else sometimes became, during his years at the university, places of evasion, comparable to movie theaters; yet, while he tended to sneak into the latter, he would enter his various jukebox cafés in a more carefree manner, telling himself that these proven places of self-reflection were also the right places for studying. This turned out to be a delusion, for once he was alone again, for instance before bedtime, and tried to review the material he had gone over in such a public setting, as a rule he had not retained much. What he owed to those niches or hideouts during the cold years of his university studies were experiences that he now, in the process of writing about them, could only characterize as "wonderful." One evening in late winter he was sitting in one of his trusty jukebox cafés, underlining a text all the more heavily the less he was taking it in. This café was in a rather untypical location for such places, at the edge of the city park, and its glass display cases with pastries and its marble-topped tables were also incongruous. The box was playing, but he was waiting as usual for the songs he had selected; only then was it right. Suddenly, after the pause between records, which, along with those noises—clicking, a whirring sound of searching back and forth through the belly of the device, snapping, swinging into place, a crackle before the first measure—constituted the essence of the jukebox, as it were, a kind of music came swelling out of the depths that made him experience, for the first time in his life, as later only in moments of love, what is technically referred to as "levitation," and which he himself, more than a quarter of a century later, would call—what? "epiphany"? "ecstasy"? "fusing with the world"? Or thus: "That—this song, this sound—is now me; with these voices; these harmonies, I have become, as never before in life, who I am: as this song is, so am I, complete!"? (As usual there was an expression for it, but as usual it was not quite the same thing: "He became one with the music.")

Without at first wanting to know the identity of the group whose voices, carried by the guitars, streamed forth singly, in counterpoint, and finally in unison—previously he had preferred soloists on jukeboxes—he was simply filled with amazement. In the following weeks, too, when he went to the place every day for hours, to sit surrounded by this big yet so frivolous sound that he let the other patrons offer him, he remained in a state of amazement devoid of name-curiosity. (Imperceptibly the music box had become the hub of the Park Café, where previously the most prominent sound had been the rattle of newspaper holders, and the only records that were played, over and over, were the two by that no-name group.) But then, when he discovered one day, during his now infrequent listening to the radio, what that choir of sassy angelic tongues was called, who, with their devil-may-care bellowing of "I Want to Hold Your Hand," "Love Me Do," "Roll Over, Beethoven," lifted all the weight in the world from his shoulders, these became the first "non-serious" records he bought (subsequently he bought hardly any other kind), and then in the café with columns he was the one who kept pushing the same buttons for "I Saw Her Standing There" (on the jukebox, of course) and "Things We Said Today" (by now without looking, the numbers and letters more firmly fixed in his head than the Ten Commandments), until one day the wrong songs, spurious voices, came nattering out: the management had left the old label and slipped in the "current hit," in German . . . And to this day, he thought, with the sound of the early Beatles in his ear, coming from that Wurlitzer surrounded by the trees in the park: when would the world see such loveliness again?

In the years that followed, jukeboxes lost some of their magnetic attraction for him—perhaps less because he now was more likely to listen to music at home, and surely not because he was getting older, but—as he thought he recognized when he got down to work on the "essay"— because he had meanwhile been living abroad. Of course he always popped in a coin whenever he encountered— in Düsseldorf, Amsterdam, Cockfosters, Santa Teresa Gallura—one of these old friends, eager to be of service, humming and sparkling with color, but it was more out of habit or tradition, and he tended to listen with only half an ear. But its significance promptly returned during his brief stopovers in what should have been his ancestral region. Whereas some people on a trip home go first "to the cemetery," "down to the lake," or "to their favorite café," he not infrequently made his way straight from the bus station to a music box, in hopes that, properly permeated with its roar, he could set out on his other visits, seeming less foreign and maladroit.

Yet there were also stories to tell of jukeboxes abroad that had played not only their records but also a role at the heart of larger events. Each of these events had occurred not just abroad but at a border: at the end of a familiar sort of world. If America was, so to speak, the "home of the jukebox," when he was there none had made much of an impression on him—except, and there time and again, in Alaska. But: did he consider Alaska part of the "United States"? — One Christmas Eve he had arrived in Anchorage, and after midnight Mass, when outside the door of the little wooden church, amid all the strangers, him included, a rare cheerfulness had taken hold, he had gone to a bar. There, in the dimness and confusion of the drunken patrons, he saw, by the glowing jukebox, the only calm figure, an Indian woman. She had turned toward him, a large, proud yet mocking face, and this would be the only time he ever danced with someone to the pounding of a jukebox. Even those patrons who were looking for a fight made way for them, as if this woman, young, or rather ageless, as she was, were the elder in that setting. Later the two of them had gone out together through a back door, where, in an icy lot, her Land Cruiser was parked, the side windows painted with Alaska pines silhouetted on the shores of an empty lake. It was snowing. From a distance, without their having touched each other except in the light-handedness of dancing, she invited him to come with her; she and her parents had a fishing business in a village beyond Cook Inlet. And in this moment it became clear to him that for once in his life there was a decision imagined not by him alone but by someone else; and at once he could imagine moving with the strange woman beyond the border out there in the snow, in complete seriousness, for good, without return, and giving up his name, his type of work, every one of his habits; those eyes there, that place, often dreamed of, far from all that was familiar—it was the moment when Percival hovered on the verge of the question that would prove his salvation, and he? on the verge of the corresponding Yes. And like Percival, and not because he was uncertain—he had that image, after all—but as if it were innate and quite proper, he hesitated, and in the next moment the image, the woman, had literally vanished into the snowy night. For the next few evenings he kept going back to the place again and again, and waited for her by the jukebox, then even made inquiries and tried to track her down, but although many remembered her, no one could tell him where she lived. Even a decade later, this experience was one of the reasons he made a point of standing in line all morning for an American

visa before flying back from Japan, then actually got off
the plane in the wintry darkness of Anchorage and spent
several days wandering through the blowing snow in this
city to whose clear air and broad horizons his heart was
attached. In the meantime, nouvelle cuisine had even
reached Alaska, and the "saloon" had turned into a "bis-
tro," with the appropriate menu, a rise in status that
naturally, and this was to be observed not only in Anchorage, left no room for a heavy, old-fashioned music
machine amid all the bright, light furniture. But an in-
dication that one might be present were the figures—of
all races—staggering onto the sidewalk from a tubelike
barracks, as if from its most remote corner, or outside,
among hunks of ice, a person surrounded by a police
patrol and flailing around—as a rule, a white male—
who then, lying on his stomach on the ground, his shoulders and his shins, bent back against his thighs, tightly
tied, his hands cuffed behind his back, was slid like a sled
along the ice and snow to the waiting police van. Inside
the barracks, one could count on being greeted right up
front at the bar, on which rested the heads of dribbling
and vomiting sleepers (men and women, mostly Eskimos),
by a classic jukebox, dominating the long tube of a room,
with the corresponding old faithfuls—one would find all
the singles of Creedence Clearwater Revival, and then
hear John Fogerty's piercing, gloomy laments cut through
the clouds of smoke—somewhere in the course of his
minstrel's wandering, he had "lost the connection," and
"If I at least had a dollar for every song I've sung!" while
from down at the railroad station, open in winter only

for freight, the whistle of a locomotive, with the odd name for the far north of Southern Pacific Railway, sends its single, prolonged organ note through the whole city, and from a wire in front of the bridge to the boat harbor, open only in summer, dangles a strangled crow.

Did this suggest that music boxes were something for idlers, for those who loafed around cities, and, in their more modern form, around the world? — No. He, at any rate, sought out jukeboxes less in times of idleness than when he had work, or plans, and particularly after returning from all sorts of foreign parts to the place he came from. The equivalent of walking out to find silence before the hours spent writing was, afterwards, almost as regularly, going to a jukebox. — For distraction? — No. When he was on the track of something, the last thing in the world he wanted was to be distracted from it. Over time his house had in fact become a house without music, without a record player and the like; whenever the news on the radio was followed by music, of whatever kind, he would turn it off; also, when time hung heavy, in hours of emptiness and dulled senses, he had only to imagine sitting in front of the television instead of alone, and he would prefer his present state. Even movie theaters, which in earlier days had been a sort of shelter after work, he now avoided more and more. By now he was too often overcome, especially in them, by a sense of being lost to the world, from which he feared he would never emerge and never find his way back to his own concerns, and that he left in the middle of the film was simply running away from such afternoon nightmares. — So he went to jukeboxes in order to collect himself, as at the beginning? — That wasn't it anymore, either. Perhaps he, who in the course of the weeks in Soria had tried to puzzle out the writings of Teresa of Avila, could explain "going to sit" with these objects after sitting at his desk by a somewhat cocky comparison: the saint had been influenced by a religious controversy of her times, at the beginning of the sixteenth century, between two groups, having to do with the best way to move closer to God. One group—the so-called *recogidos*—believed they were supposed to "collect" themselves by contracting their muscles and such, and the others—*dejados*, "leavers," or "relaxers"—simply opened themselves up passively to whatever God wanted to work in their soul, their *alma*. And Teresa of Avila seemed to be closer to the leavers than to the collectors, for she said that when someone set out to give himself more to God, he could be overwhelmed by the evil spirit—and so he sat by his jukeboxes, so to speak, not to gather concentration for going back to work, but to relax for it. Without his doing anything but keeping an ear open for the special jukebox chords—"special," too, because here, in a public place, he was not exposed to them but had chosen them, was "playing" them himself, as it were—the continuation took shape in him, as he let himself go: images that had long since become lifeless now began to move, needed only to be written down, as next to (in Spanish *junto*, attached to) the music box he was listening to Bob Marley's "Redemption Song." And from Alice's "Una notte speciale," played day after day, among other things, an entirely unplanned woman character entered the story on which he was working, and developed in all directions. And unlike after having too much to drink, the things he noted down after such listening still had substance the next day. So in those periods of reflection (which never proved fertile at home, when he tried, at his desk, to force them; he was acquainted with intentional thinking only in the form of making comparisons and distinctions), he would set out not only to walk as far as possible but also out to the jukebox joints. When he was sitting in the pimps' hangout, whose box had once been shot at, or in the café of the unemployed, with its table for patients out on passes from the nearby mental hospital—silent, expressionless palefaces, in motion only for swallowing pills with beer—no one wanted to believe him that he had come not for the atmosphere but to hear "Hey Joe" and "Me and Bobby McGee" again. — But didn't that mean that he sought out jukeboxes in order to, as people said, sneak away from the present? — Perhaps. Yet as a rule the opposite was true: with his favorite object there, anything else around acquired a presentness all its own. Whenever possible, he would find a seat in such joints from which he could see the entire room and a bit of the outside. Here he would often achieve, in consort with the jukebox, along with letting his imagination roam, and without engaging in the observing he found so distasteful, a strengthening of himself, or an immersion in the present, which applied to the other sights as well. And what became present about them was not so much their striking features or their particular attractions as their ordinary aspects, even just the familiar forms or colors, and such enhanced presentness seemed valuable to him—nothing more precious or more worthy of being passed on than this; a sort of heightened awareness such as otherwise occurs only with a book that stimulates reflection. So it *meant* something, quite simply, when a man left, a branch stirred, the bus was yellow and turned off at the station, the intersection formed a triangle, the chalk was lying at the edge of the pool table, it was raining, and, and, and. Yes, that was it: the present was equipped with flexible joints! Thus, even the little habits of "us jukebox players" deserved attention, along with the few variations. While he himself usually propped one hand on his hip while he pushed the buttons, and leaned forward a little, almost touching the thing, another person stood some distance away, legs spread, arms outstretched like a technician; and a third let his fingers rebound from the buttons like a pianist, then immediately went away, sure of the result, or remained, as if waiting for the outcome of an experiment, until the sound came (and then perhaps disappeared without listening to any more, out onto the street), or as a matter of principle had all his songs selected by others, to whom he called out from his table the codes, which he knew by heart. What they all had in common was that they seemed to see the jukebox as a sort of living thing, a pet: "Since yesterday she hasn't been quite right." "I dunno what's wrong with her today; she's acting crazy." — So was one of these devices just like any other, as far as he was concerned? — No. There were telling differences, ranging from clear aversion to downright tenderness or actual reverence. — Toward a mass-produced object? — Toward the human touches in it. The form of the device itself mattered less and less for him as time went on. As far as he was concerned, the jukebox could be a wartime product made of wood, or could be called—instead of Wurlitzer—Music Chest, or Symphony, or Fanfare, and such a product of the German economic miracle could look like a small box, even have no lights at all, be made of dark, opaque glass, silent and to all appearances out of commission, but then the list of selections would light up once you put the coin in, and after you pushed the buttons that internal whirring would begin, accompanied by the selector light on the black glass front. Not even the characteristic jukebox sound was so decisive for him anymore, emanating from the depths as from under many soundless layers, the unique roaring that could often be heard only if one listened for it, similar, he thought one time, to the way the "river" in William Faulkner's story can be heard far below the silent, standing ocean waters in the land the river has flooded from horizon to horizon, as the "roaring of the Mississippi." In a pinch, he could make do with a wall box, where the sound came out flatter, or more tinny, than it ever had from a transistor radio, and if absolutely necessary, if there was so much noise in the place that the actual sound of the music became inaudible, even a certain rhythmic vibration sufficed; he could then make out the chorus or even just one measure—his only requirement—of the music he had selected, from which the whole song would play in his ear, from vibration to vibration. But he disliked those music boxes where the choice of songs, instead of being unique and "personally" put together at that location, was itself mass-produced, the same from one place to the next throughout an entire country, without variation, and made available to the individual establishments, indeed forced on them, by an anonymous central authority, which he could picture as a sort of Mafia, the jukebox Mafia. Such unvarying, lockstep programs, with choices among only current hits, even in a fine old Wurlitzer—by now there was hardly anything else in all countries—could be recognized by the fact that there was no longer a typed list; it was printed, completely covering the slots for individual song titles and performers' names. But, strangely enough, he also avoided those jukeboxes whose list of offerings, like the menu in certain restaurants, was done in a uniform handwriting from top to bottom, from left to right, although, as a rule, precisely there every single record seemed intended for him alone; he did not like a jukebox's program to embody any plan, no matter how noble, any connoisseurship, any secret knowledge, any harmony; he wanted it to represent confusion, with an admixture of the unfamiliar (more and more as the years went by), and also plenty of pieces for escape, among them, to be sure, and all the more precious, the very songs (just a few, to be hunted down among all the chaotic possibilities, were enough) that met his needs at the moment. Such music boxes also made themselves known in their menu of choices; with a hodgepodge of machine- and handwritten notations, and, above all, handwriting

that changed from title to title, one in block letters, in
ink, the next in flowing, almost stenographic secretary
style, but most, even with the most dissimilar loops and
slants of the letters, showing signs of particular care and
seriousness, some, like children's handwriting, as if
painted, and, time and again, among all the mistakes,
correctly written ones (with proper accents and hyphens),
song titles that must have struck the waitress in question
as very foreign, the paper here and there already yellowed,
the writing faded and hard to make out, perhaps also
taped over with freshly written labels with different titles,
but where it showed through, even if illegible, still powerfully suggestive. In time, his first glance more and more
sought out those records in a jukebox's table of choices
that were indicated in such handwriting, rather than "his"
records, even if there was only one such. And sometimes
that was the only one he listened to, even if it had been
unfamiliar or completely unknown to him beforehand.
Thus, in a North African bar in a Paris suburb, standing
in front of a jukebox (whose list of exclusively French
selections immediately made it recognizable as a Mafia
product), he had discovered on the edge a label, handwritten, in very large, irregular letters, each as emphatic
as an exclamation point, and had selected that smuggled-
in Arab song, then again and again, and even now he
was still haunted by that far-resonating SIDI MANSUR,
which the bartender, rousing himself from his silence,
told him was the name of "a special, out-of-the-ordinary
place" ("You can't just go there!").

.   .   .

Was that supposed to mean that he regretted the disappearance of his jukeboxes, these objects of yesteryear, unlikely to have a second future?

No. He merely wanted to capture and acknowledge, before even he lost sight of it, what an object could mean to a person, above all what could emanate from a mere object. — An eating place by a playing field on the outskirts of Salzburg. Outdoors. A bright summer evening. The jukebox is outside, next to the open door. On the terrace, different patrons at every table, Dutch, English, Spanish, speaking their own languages, for the place also serves the adjacent campgrounds, by the airfield. It is the early eighties, the airfield has not yet become "Salzburg airport," the last plane lands at sundown. The trees between the terrace and the playing field are birches and poplars, in the warm air constant fluttering of leaves against the deep yellow sky. At one table the locals are sitting, members of the Maxglan Working Man's Athletic Club with their wives. The soccer team, at that time still a second-division club, has just lost another game that afternoon, and will probably be dropped from the league. But now, in the evening, those affected are talking about the trees for a change, while there is a constant coming and going at the window where beer is dispensed—from the tents and back. They look at the trees: how big they've gotten and how straight they've grown, since they, the club members, went out and with their own hands dug them up as seedlings from the black mossy soil and planted them here in rows in the brown clay! The song the jukebox sends out again and again that evening into the gradually oncoming darkness, in the pauses between the rustling and rasping of the leaves and the even buzz of voices, is sung in an enterprising voice by Helene Schneider, and is called "Hot Summer Nites." The place is completely empty, and the white curtains billow in at the open windows. Then at some point someone is sitting inside, in a corner, a young woman, silently weeping.

—Years later. A restaurant, a *gostilna*, on the crown of the Yugoslavian karst, at some remove from the highway from Stanjel (or San Daniele del Carso). Indoors. A mighty old-fashioned jukebox next to a cupboard, on the way to the restroom. Visible behind ornamental glass, the record carousel and turntable. To operate it, one uses tokens instead of coins, and then it is not enough to push a button, of which there is only one; first, one has to turn a dial until the desired selection lines up with the indicator arrow. The mechanical arm then places the record on the turntable with an elegance comparable to the elbow flourish with which an impeccably trained waiter presents a dish. The *gostilna* is large, with several dining rooms, which on this evening in early fall—while outside the *burja*, or *bora*, blasts without relief over the highland, coming from the mountains in the north—are full, mostly with young people: an end-of-term party for several classes from all the republics of Yugoslavia; they have met one another for the first time here, over several days. Once the wind carries the distinctive signal of the karst train down from the cliffs, with the dark sound of a mountain ferry. On the wall, across from the customary picture of Tito, hangs an equally colorful but much larger portrait of an unknown: it is the former proprietor, who took his own life. His wife says he was not from around here (even if only from the village in the next valley). The song, selected this evening by one student after another, that wafts through the dining rooms over and over again is sung in a self-conscious and at the same time childishly merry unison, even, as an expression of a people, danceable, and has one word as its refrain: "Jugoslavija!"

—Again years later. Again a summer evening, before dusk, this time on the Italian side of the karst, or, to be precise, the border of the limestone base, once heaved out of the sea, of the cliffless lowlands, here marked by the tracks of the railroad station of Monfalcone. Just beyond it, the desert of stones that rises toward the plateau, concealed along this section of track by a small pine forest —on this side the station, surrounded by the abruptly different vegetation of cedars, palms, plane trees, rhododendron, along with the requisite water, pouring plentifully from the station fountain, whose spigot no one has bothered to turn off. The jukebox stands in the bar, under the window, which is wide open after the heat of the day; likewise open, the door leading out to the tracks. Otherwise, the place is almost entirely without furniture; what little there is has been shoved to one side, and they are mopping up already. The lights of the jukebox are reflected in the wet terrazzo floor, a glow that gradually disappears as the floor dries. The face of the barmaid appears very pale at the window, in contrast to those of the few passengers waiting outside, which are tanned. After the departure of the Trieste–Venice Express, the building appears empty, except that on a bench two adolescent boys are tussling, yelling at the top of their voices; the railroad station is their playground at the moment. From the darkness of the pines of the karst, swarms of moths are issuing forth. A long, sealed freight train rattle-pounds by, the only bright spot against the outside of the cars being the little lead seals blowing behind on their cords. In the stillness that follows—it is the time between the last swallows and the first bats—the sound of the jukebox is heard. The boys tussle a bit longer. Not to listen, but probably quite by chance, two railroad officials come out of their offices to the platform, and from the waiting room comes a cleaning woman. Suddenly figures, previously overlooked, appear all over the scene. On the bench by the beech, a man is sleeping. On the grass behind the restrooms, soldiers are stretched out, a whole group, without a trace of luggage. On the platform to Udine, leaning against a pillar, a huge black man, likewise without luggage, just in shirt and pants, engrossed in a book. From the thicket of pines behind the station swoop again and again, one following close upon the other, a pair of doves. It is as if all of them were not travelers but inhabitants or settlers in the area around the railroad station. Its midpoint is the fountain, with its foaming drinking water, blown and spattered by the breeze, and tracks on the asphalt from many wet soles, to which the last drinker now intentionally adds his own. A bit farther down the tracks, accessible on foot, the subterranean karst river, the Timavo, comes to the surface, with three branches, which in Virgil's time, according to the *Æneid*, were still nine; it immediately broadens out and empties into the Mediterranean. The song the jukebox is playing tells of a letter written by a young woman who has ended up far away from her home and from everything she ever knew or dreamed of, and is now full of brave and perhaps also sorrowful astonishment; it floats out into the dusky railroad land of Monfalcone in the friendly voice of Michelle Shocked, and is called "Anchorage, Alaska."

During the weeks in Soria he sometimes managed to think this about what he was doing: "I'm doing my work. It agrees with me." Once he found himself thinking, "I have time," without the usual ulterior motives, just that one, big thought. It rained and stormed over the Castilian highland almost every day, and he used his pencils to jam the curtain into the cracks around the window. The noise still bothered him more. The fish-scaling down below, outside the kitchen door, became a daily dismembering, with a meat ax, of altogether different animals, and the agreeably looping paths out on the steppe turned out to be a motocross course. (Soria was even competing, he discovered, for the European cup.) Seen on television, this sport, with its heroes bouncing into the air like video-game figures, had something admirable about it, but now, sitting at his table, he found the buzzing of a hornet around his head a blessing by comparison. Again and again he came back from his walk filled with strength—

his own kind of strength—for work, and promptly lost it in the racket. The noise destroyed something not only for the moment but for good. The worrisome thing was that it put him at risk of disparaging an activity like his conjuring up of images and then putting them into words, which required so much solitude. On the other hand, in silence he had in fact occasionally gone astray, and now actually drew strength precisely from his weakness—his doubts, even more his hopelessness—going to work in defiance of his surroundings. Every day he traced his arc past the façade of Santo Domingo—no, in contrast to the new buildings behind it, that was no façade. Peace emanated from it; all he had to do was take it in. Amazing how the sculptures told their stories: Eve, being led to Adam by God, was already standing back-to-back with her husband in the next scene, where he gazed up at the Tree of Knowledge, and word of Christ's Resurrection, given by one of the women to the first in the long line of Apostles, was immediately passed down the row to the end, as one could see from the body language; only the last in line, motionless, seemed not to have heard yet.

Before work he walked with short steps, afterwards with longer ones, not out of a sense of triumph, but because he was dizzy. Going up the mountainside made him breathe more deeply and think more clearly, but it could not be too steep, or his thoughts would grow too agitated. Likewise, he preferred going upstream to the other direction; there was an element of forging one's way, with the energy that produced. If he wanted to keep from brooding, he walked along the ties of the abandoned rail line that had linked Soria and Burgos, or went even farther out of town into the darkness, where he had to watch where he put his feet. When he returned from the darkness of the steppe to town, he was so tense from groping his way along that he felt like having the playful figures of Santo Domingo loosen him up and smooth the tightness from his face. He repeated the same routes, just adding a variation every day; yet it seemed to him as if all the other paths were waiting to be taken. Along Antonio Machados's promenade lay years' worth of tissues and condoms. During the day there were, besides him, almost exclusively old men out in the steppes, usually alone, with worn shoes; before they blew their noses, they ceremoniously pulled out their handkerchiefs and shook them. Before work, he made a point of saying hello to at least one of them, intending to be greeted in turn; he did not want to go back to his room without having experienced this moment of smiling; sometimes he even stopped just for that purpose and let one of them catch up with him, so as to get in the *"Hola!"* and the jerk of the head. Before that, he read the paper every day, by a large window in Soria's Central Bar, with the help of a dictionary. *Llavero* meant a "bunch of keys": with a raised bunch of keys a woman took part in a demonstration in Prague; *dedo pulgar* meant thumb: the American President gave the thumbs-up sign to indicate the successful bloodletting in Panama; *puerta giratoria* meant a revolving door (through which Samuel Beckett in his time had entered the Closerie des Lilas in Paris). The news of the

execution of the Ceauçescu couple he read not with sat-
isfaction but with an old, newly reawakened horror of
history. When time allowed, he continued to decipher the
characters of Theophrastus, and came to feel fond of many
of them, at least in some of their traits—which he perhaps
recognized as his own. It seemed to him that their weak-
nesses and foolishness were indications of lonely people
who could not fit in with society, in this case the Greek
polis, and in order to be part of it in some way played
their ludicrous game with the courage born of desperation; if they were overzealous, unsuitably youthful, boast-
ful, or, more revealingly, always "in the wrong place at
the wrong time," the explanation was often simply that
they could not find their niche among the others, even
their children and slaves. Occasionally he would look up
and gaze out the window at a plane tree—still with its
withered foliage—and next to it an already completely
bare mountain maple, in which, almost predictably, except
in a violent storm, the sparrows would be perched like
buds, so quiet that the whipping, flapping, swirling jagged
leaves next to them were more like birds than they were.
He experienced his most powerful sense of place down
by the bridge that spanned the river, less at the sight of
the stone arches and the dark winter water flowing past
than of the sign at the highest point of the bridge: RIO
DUERO. One of the bars down by the water was called
Alegría del Puente, Joy of the Bridge, and when he read
the sign he immediately took the detour, the *rodeo*, to go
in. Along the riverbanks, where they were not sheer cliffs,
smooth-polished glacial boulders protruded from the

earth, and on the remains of the city walls, far out in the
steppe, the wind of the centuries had ridged, striped,
pitted, patterned the yellow sandstone, and he saw several
old palaces on the Plaza Mayor built on foundations of
pebbles naturally cemented at the bottom of glacial lakes.
To be able to read the landscape a little in passing
grounded one, and he learned that in Spain geography
had always been subservient to history, to conquests and
border drawings, and only now was more attention being
paid to the "messages of places." Sometimes colors were
particularly alive in winter. While the sky looked sulfurous, a fallow field down below was greening up, and the
paths through the rock-strewn fields also showed mossy
green. Where everything else had long since faded, a
rosebush covered with hips formed a glowing red arch.
A pair of magpies fluttered up, their wings brightening
the air like rapidly turning wheels. On a day when it was
not raining, little puffs of dust sprang up around the town,
and he got a feel for summer in these parts. The shadows
of clouds passed over the bare highland, as if pulled from
underground—as if there were cloud shadows everywhere, but their home was here in Castile. One morning
there was an hour without wind for a change, and in the
clear sun both the northern and the eastern sierra could
be seen with snow cover for the first time, and although
both mountain chains were a small airplane journey away,
he saw the sparkling slopes checkered by cloud shadows,
motionless, for the duration of that hour without wind.
In his thoughts he was so preoccupied with the snow that
he involuntarily stamped it off his shoes when he reached

his door. A few times, when he was groping his way across the deserted area outside town (he sent himself there for this very purpose), the night sky cleared up briefly, and the effect was all the more amazing when Castor and Pollux showed their fraternal distance, Venus glittered, Aldebaran sparkled in Arabic fashion, the W of Cassiopeia formed wide thighs, the Big Dipper bent its handle, and Lepus, the hare, in flight from the hunter Orion, dashed horizontally across the firmament. The Milky Way with its numerous Delta branches was a pale reflection of the universe's initial explosion. Strange, the feeling of having a "long time" during this December in Soria: already, after the first day spent writing, when he caught sight of the river down there, he found himself thinking, "There he is, the good old Duero!" When one weekend he had not made his rounds past the Río Bar, he felt, back by its little cast-iron stove, as if he had not visited this gray cylinder "in ages." Scarcely a week after his arrival, he thought, as he wandered past the bus station: "This is where I stepped out into the rain with my suitcase that time!" In the midst of a roaring gale, a toad lurching through the steppe grass. Before the plane tree's leaves dropped, their stems broke, became fringed, spun on the fringes. When the cock was in the muddy garden where the unripe tomatoes were left as feed, did his tail feathers move of their own accord, or was that the wind? But his true heraldic animals were those dogs he saw wandering around in the evening, limping on three legs: at the end of his day's journey, one of his knees usually gave out, too. Once, when according to the paper Soria was not the coldest town in Spain, he felt disappointed. Once, on the main street, a pot with a red poinsettia was carried along, beneath the green, still not fallen, always wet leaves of the plane trees; not once in those weeks did the puddles in the hollows around the roots evaporate. The fog was dark gray, and against that background the many white cocoons of the needle-eating processionary moths stood out all the more menacingly in the mountain pines. On Christmas Day it rained so hard that, during his usual walk through town, besides him only a solitary sparrow seemed to be on the street. Then, from the county jail, without an umbrella, emerged a very small woman and her big son and crossed the sea of mud to a temporary barracks set up there, and he imagined that behind the high walls they had just visited a relative, one of the Basques on a hunger strike, and were camping out here until he was freed. In the evening there was a sudden flash of light between torrents of rain, and something hit him on his forehead and chin, and when he looked around, he saw a car with its roof all white coming from out of town, and way up in the black of night a few flakes began to float as they fell: *"Nieve!"* he thought, his first spontaneous word in Spanish. In a bar they struck up a flamenco song, for once without the usual gypsy-like note of futility, but cheerful, confident, with the air of a herald, and a notion ran through his mind: here, finally, was the appropriate way to sing for—not Christmas, but *Navidad*, the birth; this was how one of the shepherds would describe what he had seen in that holy night, and his description was of course also a dance. Here, as everywhere in the world, he saw passersby who, at the first drops of rain, put up the umbrellas they always had with them, and even here on the *meseta* it was the fashion for young girls, when they entered a restaurant, to blow their bangs off their foreheads. Thunderous wind, like an airplane taking off (actually, something one almost never heard over the city), in the poplars along the Duero. A large hen tenderly groomed the comb of a little rooster, standing on one leg in the muck. In a bare almond tree there was already one branch with white flower buds. Most of the evils with which he was familiar from his accustomed surroundings, including those within him, remained at a distance here, housed as he was once again by his work, and yet, in the long run, a sense of life—this he recognized in Soria—could not come from what was absent. Hoarfrost lay on the tree roots that terraced steps into a path. One time, as he sat at his table, something outside detonated and he heard it as a temple bell.

In the end he believed he had explored almost every corner of the city (he memorized these *rincones* as if they were vocabulary words). He entered almost a hundred buildings, for, as he discovered in the course of his conscientious wanderings, little Soria had well over a hundred bars, off the beaten track, in alleys between buildings, often without signs, hidden, like so many things in Spanish towns, from casual glances and known only to those who lived there—as if reserved for them alone. Again and again he found on walls, along with the announcements about hunting times and the pictures of toreros, poems by An-

tonio Machado, also as wall calendars, some with graffiti
on them, one even with a swastika, yet, it seemed to him,
not for the usual reasons, but because the poems, at least
those chosen as wall decorations, had to do with nature.
Amazing how in many establishments there were only
young people, and how there were even more bars for
older people exclusively and explicitly closed to anyone
else (with a table in the corner for the old women): to all
appearances, a stricter separation than any political one.
Most of the retirees in the province spent their "golden"
years here in the capital, and when they were not playing
cards in their bars, they sat quietly by themselves at a
table or fumbled and poked around incessantly, searching
for something. Young and old and he, the stranger in the
land, in addition: all their wintry hands lay equally pale
on the counters, while the glow of the streetlights outside
showed up, for example, the scars on a concrete wall left
by a falling metal scaffolding that had killed two pedes-
trians back when he arrived.

Besides his pleasure in the variations in these places that
appeared so similar, he also felt particularly driven to find
a jukebox in Soria, first probably out of the old compulsion, but later more and more because this would have
been the proper time for it: work, winter, the evenings
after the long walks in the pouring rain. Once, already
far out along the *carretera* to Valladolid, he heard from
a bar along the highway a deep sound that then turned
out to belong to a pinball machine decorated like a chamber of horrors; in a gas-station bar he saw the sign

WURLITZER—on a cigarette machine; in a building being torn down in the *casco*, the center of Soria, surrounded by craters of rubble, he caught sight, in the Andalusian-style tiled bar there, of the selection chart from an ancient Marconi apparatus, a forerunner of the jukebox, used as wall decoration. The only time he laid eyes on his object in Soria was in the Rex movie theater, in an English film set in the early sixties: there it stood, in a back room, waiting for the moment when the hero went by on his way to the men's room. The only living jukebox in Spain, so to speak, remained for him the one from Linares, in Andalusia. At that time, too, in the spring, he had needed it: work, the commotion of Easter Week. That jukebox, which he had come upon only shortly before leaving, the search long since abandoned, greeted him in a cellar off a side street. A place the size of a storeroom, no windows, only the door. Open at irregular times, and, when open, only in the evening, but then the sign was often not lit —you had to try the door to see if anything was going on there. The proprietor, an old man (turning on the ceiling light only when a guest arrived), usually alone with the jukebox. This one had the unusual feature that all the selection tabs were blank, like nameplates in a high-rise apartment house with all the names missing; like the entire place, it seemed to be out of service; only the alphanumeric codes at the beginning of the blank tabs. But all over the wall, in every direction, up to the ceiling, record covers were tacked, with the proper codes written on them by hand, and thus, after the machine had been switched on, each time only on request, the desired record—the belly of the seemingly disemboweled object turned out to be chock-full of them—could be set in motion. Suddenly there was so much space in that little hovel from the monotonous thumping deep inside the steel, so much peace emanated from that place, in the midst of the hectic Spanish pace and his own. That was on the Calle Cervantes of Linares, with the abandoned movie theater across the street, with remains of a sign reading *Estreno,* premiere, and bundles of newspapers and rats in the barred lobby, at a time when on the steppes outside the city the hard-headed steppe chamomile was in bloom, and more than thirty years after Manuel Rodríguez, called Manolete, was gored to death by a bull in the arena at Linares. A few steps below the bar, which was called El Escudo, the Escutcheon, was Linares's Chinese restaurant, sometimes a place of peace for a person from elsewhere, like the jukebox. In Soria, too, he discovered, to his surprise, a seemingly hidden Chinese restaurant; it looked closed, yet the door sprang open, and when he stepped inside, the large paper lanterns were switched on. He remained the only diner that evening. In town he had never seen the Asian family that ate here at the long table in the corner and then disappeared into the kitchen. Only the girl stayed behind and served him in silence. On the walls, pictures of the Great Wall, from which the place took its name. Strange, how when he dipped his porcelain spoon into the bowl with the dark soup, the bright heads of the beansprouts popped up, here in the Castilian highlands, like figures in an animated cartoon, while in the nightly storm outside the window the poplar branches clicked. The young girl, otherwise idle, was painting Chinese letters into a notebook at the next table, one close to the other, in a writing far more even than his own during these weeks (not only the storm gusts, the rain, and the darkness when he took notes outdoors, since he had been at work, had ruined it), and as he kept watching her, who had to feel incomparably more foreign than he did in this area, in this Spain, he sensed with amazement that he had only now really set out from the place he came from.

ESSAY

ON

THE

SUCCESSFUL

DAY

———

Translated by

Ralph Manheim

A self-portrait by William Hogarth, an eighteenth-century moment, showing a palette divided approximately in the middle by a gently curving line, the so-called Line of Beauty and Grace. And on my desk a flat, rounded stone found on the shore of Lake Constance, dark granite, traversed diagonally by a vein of chalky white, with a subtle, almost playful bend, deviating from the straight line at exactly the right moment and dividing the stone into two halves, while at the same time holding it together. And that trip in a suburban train through the hills to the west of Paris, at the afternoon hour when as a rule the fresh air and clean light of certain early-morning departures are vitiated, when nothing is natural any longer and it seems likely that only the coming of darkness can bring relief from the closeness of the day, then suddenly the tracks swing out in a wide arc, strangely, breathtakingly high above the city, which unexpectedly, along with the crazy reality of its enigmatic structures, opens out into the fluvial plain—there on the heights of Saint-Cloud or Suresnes, with that unforeseen curve, an instant transition changed the course of my day, and my almost abandoned idea of a "successful day" was back again, accompanied by a heartwarming impulse to describe, list, or discuss the elements of such a day and the problems it raises. The Line of Beauty and Grace on Hogarth's palette seems literally to force its way through the formless masses of paint, seems to cut between them and yet to cast a shadow.

Who has ever experienced a successful day? Most people will say without thinking that they have. But then it will be necessary to ask: Do you mean "successful" or only "happy"? Are you thinking of a successful day or only of a "carefree" one, which admittedly is just as unusual. If a day goes by without confronting you with problems, does that, in your opinion, suffice to make it a successful day? Do you see a distinction between a happy day and a successful one? Is it essentially different to speak of some successful day in the past, with the help of memory, and right now after the day, which no intervening time has transfigured, to say not that a day has been "dealt with" or "got out of the way," but that it has been "successful"? To your mind, is a successful day basically different from a carefree or happy day, from a full or busy day, a day struggled through, or a day transfigured by the distant past—one particular suffices, and a whole day rises up in glory—perhaps even some Great Day for Science, your country, our people, the peoples of the earth, mankind? (And that reminds me: Look—look up—the outline of that bird up there in the tree; translated literally, the Greek verb for "read," used in the Pauline epistles, would signify a "looking up," even a "perceiving *upward*" or "recognizing *upward*," a verb without special imperative form, but in itself a summons, an appeal; and then those hummingbirds in the jungles of South America, which in leaving their sheltering tree imitate the wavering of a falling leaf to mislead the hawk . . .) —Yes, to me a successful day is not the same as any other; it *means* more. A successful day is more. It is more than a "successful remark," more than a "successful chess move" (or even a whole successful game), more than a "successful first winter ascent," than a "successful flight," a "successful operation," a "successful relationship," or any "successful piece of business"; it is independent of a successful brush-stroke or sentence, nor should it be confused with some "poem, which after a lifetime of waiting achieved success in a single hour." The successful day is incomparable. It is unique.

It is symptomatic of our particular epoch that the success of a single day can become a "subject" (or a reproach). Consider that in times gone by more importance was attached to faith in a correctly chosen moment, which could indeed stand for the whole of life. Faith? Belief? Idea? In the remote past, at all events, regardless of whether you were herding sheep on the slopes of Pindus, strolling about below the Acropolis, or building a wall on the stony plateau of Arcadia, you had to reckon with a god of the right moment or time-atom, a god in any case. And in its day, no doubt, this god of the moment was more powerful than all seemingly immutable embodiments of gods—always present, always here, always valid. But in the end he, too, was dethroned—or, who knows?—mightn't it have been your god of "now!" (*and*

of the eyes that meet, and of the sky which, formless only
a moment ago, suddenly took on form, *and* of the water-
smooth stone, which suddenly showed the play of its
colors, *and, and*) that was dethroned by the faith that came
after—no longer image or idea, but faith "born of love"
in a new Creation, in which all moments and epochs are
fulfilled through the Incarnation, death, and Resurrection
of the Son of God, and thus in so-called eternity, a gospel
whose missionaries proclaimed first that it was not made
to the measure of man, and second that those who believed
in it would transcend the mere moments of philosophy
and enjoy the aeons, or, rather, the eternities of religion.
There then followed, distinct from both the god of the
moment and the God of eternity, though without suffi-
cient zeal to demolish the one or the other, a period of
purely immanent, or, to state it plainly, secular power,
which put its reliance—your kairos-cult, your Greeks,
your heavenly beatitude, your Christians and Muslims
mean nothing to me—on something intermediary, on
the success of my here-and-now, of the successful individual lifetime. Faith? Dream? Vision? Most likely—at
least at the start of this period—a vision: the vision of
people who have been disillusioned with all faith of any
kind; a sort of defiant daydream. Since nothing outside
me is thinkable, I will make the utmost of my life. Thus
the era of this third power was superlative in word and
deed: labors of Hercules, world movements. "Was"? Does
it follow that this era is past? No, the idea of a whole life
made successful by activity is of course still in force and
will always remain fruitful. But apparently there is little

more to be said about it, for the epics and romances of
adventure of the pioneers, who resolutely lived the original dream of the active life, have already been told and
provide the models for today's successful lives—each one
a variant of the well-known formula: Plant a tree, get a
child, write a book—and all that's left to talk about are
strange little variations or glosses, tossed off at random,
something for example about a young man of thirty, mar-
ried to a woman whom he was confident of loving to the
end, a teacher at a small suburban school, to whose
monthly magazine he contributed occasional theater or
movie notes, who had no further plans for the future (no
tree, no book, no child), telling friends, not only since the
completion of his thirtieth year, but on his last few birth-
days as well, with festively lit-up eyes, of his certainty that
his life had been successful (the words sound even weirder
in the French original, "j'ai réussi ma vie"—"I've made
a good thing of my life"?). Was the epochal vision of the
successful life still at work in this man of today? Was his
statement still an expression of faith? It is a long time
since those words were spoken, but in my imagination,
regardless of what may have happened to the man since,
I feel sure that if anyone asks him he will still automatically give the same reply. So it must be faith. What sort
of faith? —What can have become of that young "successful life"?

Do you mean to imply that, unlike successful lives, your
so-called successful day is more meaningful today than
any mere glosses or copies or travesties? Is it so very

different from the motto from the Golden Age of Rome, "carpe diem," which today, two thousand years later, can serve equally well as a brand of wine, an inscription on a T-shirt, or the name of a nightclub. (Once again it all depends on how you translate it: "Make the best of your day"—as it was understood in the century of action—? "Gather the day"—whereby the day becomes one great favorable moment—? or "Let the day bear fruit"— whereby Horace's famous dictum suddenly comes close to my today-problem—?) And what is a successful day anyway—because thus far you have only been trying to make clear what it is not? But with all your digressions, complications, and tergiversations, your way of breaking off every time you gain a bit of momentum, what becomes of your Line of Beauty and Grace, which, as you've hinted, stands for a successful day and, as you went on to assure us, would introduce your essay on the subject. When will you abandon your irresolute peripheral zigzags, your timorous attempt to define a concept that seems to be growing emptier than ever, and at last, with the help of coherent sentences, make the light, sharp incision that will carry us through the present muddle and in medias res, in the hope that this obscure "successful day" of yours may take on clarity and universal form. How do you conceive of such a day? Give me a rough sketch of it, show me a picture of it. Tell me about this successful day. Show me the dance of the successful day. Sing me the song of the successful day!

•   •   •

There really is a song that might have been called "A Successful Day." It was sung by Van Morrison, my favorite singer (or one of them), and it actually has a different title, the name of a small American town that is otherwise of no interest. It tells the story in pictures of a car ride on a Sunday—when a successful day seems even more unlikely than on any other day of the week—for two, a man and a woman, no doubt, in the we-form (in which the success of a day seems an even greater event than for one person alone): fishing in the mountains, driving on, buying the Sunday paper, driving on, a snack, driving on, the shimmer of your hair, arriving in the evening, with roughly this last line: "Why can't every day be like this?" It's a very short song, maybe the shortest ballad ever, it hardly takes a minute, and the man who sings it is almost elderly, with a few last strands of hair, and it talks more than it sings about that day, without tune or resonance, in a kind of casual murmur, but out of a broad, powerful chest, suddenly breaking off just as it swells its widest.

Nowadays, the Line of Beauty and Grace might be unlikely to take the same gentle curve as in Hogarth's eighteenth century, which, at least in prosperous, self-sufficient England, conceived of itself as a very earthly epoch. Isn't it typical of people like us that this sort of song keeps breaking off, lapsing into stuttering, babbling, and silence, starting up again, going off on a sidetrack—yet in the end, as throughout, aiming at unity and wholeness? And isn't it equally typical of us late-twentieth-century people that we think about a single successful day rather than some sort of eternity or an entire successful life—no, not only in the sense of "Live in the present," and certainly not of "Gather ye rosebuds," but also in the urgent, needful hope that by investigating the elements of this one period of time one might devise a model for a greater, still greater, if not the greatest possible period, because now that all the old ideas of time have gone up in smoke, this drifting from day to day without rule or precept (except perhaps with reference to what one should *not* do in one's lifetime), devoid of ties (with you, with that passerby) or the slightest certainty (that the present moment of joy will be repeated tomorrow if ever), though bearable in youth, when it may even be accompanied or encouraged by carefreeness, gives way in time to more frequent dissatisfaction and, with advancing age, to indignation. And since age, unlike youth, cannot rebel against heaven, against present conditions on earth, or anything else, my indignation turns against myself. Damn it, why aren't we together anymore? Why at three o'clock this afternoon has the light in the country lane, or the clatter of the train wheels, or your face ceased to be the event it was this morning and promised to remain forever and ever. Damn it, why, quite unlike what is supposed to happen as one grows older, am I less able than ever to remember, hold fast, and treasure the moments of my life? Damn it, why am I so scatterbrained? Damn, damn, damn. (And while we're at it, look at those gym shoes drying on the windowsill of the gabled house across the street; they belong

to the neighbor kid we saw last night in the floodlight of
the makeshift football field, plucking at the seam of his
jersey while running to intercept a pass.)

So, to judge by what you say about the successful moment,
the successful life, whether eternal or individual, you regard the idea of the successful day as a kind of fourth
power. And that leads you to endow this successful day
with a fragrance that will never evaporate but, regardless
of what may happen to you tomorrow, will somehow
linger on. Thus it is time to ask once again: "How precisely do you envision a successful day?" I can give you
no precise picture of a successful day. I have only the idea,
and I almost despair of showing you a recognizable con-
tour, bringing out the design, or tracing the original light
trail of my day, or disclosing it in simple purity, as I
longed to do at the start. Since there is nothing but the
idea, the idea is all I can tell you about. "I'd like to tell
you an idea." But how can an idea be told? There came
a jolt (the "ugliness" of this word has often been held up
to me, but once again there is no other way of saying it).
It grew light? It widened? It took hold of me? It vibrated?
It blew warm? It cleared? It was day again at the end of
the day? No, the idea resists my narrative urge. It provides
me with no picture to serve as an excuse. And yet it was
corporeal, more corporeal than any image or representation has ever been; it synthesized all the body's dispersed
senses into energy. Idea means this: It provided no picture,
only light. This idea was not recollection of well-spent
childhood days; it cast its beam exclusively forward, on

the future. If it can be told, then only in the future form, a future story, such as "On a successful day, day will dawn again at noon. It will give me a jolt, two jolts: one pressing me onward, the other reaching deep inside me. At the end of the successful day, I shall have the effrontery to say that for once I had lived as one should live—with an effrontery corresponding to my innate reserve." No, the idea was not about childhood days, the days of yore; it was about a grownup day, a future day, and the idea was in reality an action, it acted, intervened beyond the simple future, as a hortative form, with the help of which, for example, Van Morrison's song might be rendered more or less as follows: "On the successful day, the Catskill Mountains should be the Catskills, the turn-off to the rest area should be the turn-off to the rest area, the Sunday paper should be the Sunday paper, nightfall should be nightfall, your radiance beside me should . . ." Of course, but how is that sort of thing to be brought about? Will my own dance be enough? Or should it be "Anmut" or "Grazia" or "Gnade" instead of "Grace"? And what does it signify that the time when the idea of the successful day first crossed my mind was not a long period of near-despair? The monster of speechlessness has given way to silence. In broad daylight his dream about the bird's nest made of hay, flat on the ground, with the naked, cheeping chicks in it, recurred. The particles of mica in the stone sidewalk glittered close to my eyes. His memory of his mother's warmth that day when she gave him all the money she had for a new watch strap, and his memory of the maxim: "God loveth a cheerful giver." The flying

---

blackbird's wing that grazed the hedge far down the road grazed him at the same time. On the asphalt platform of the Issy–Plaine station the overlapping marks of a thousand different shoe soles imprinted by yesterday's rain have now dried into a lighter color. As he passed the unknown child, the child's cowlick repeated itself in his mind. The steeple of Saint-Germain-des-Prés, across from the cafés, the bookshop, the salon de coiffure, and the pharmacy, was simultaneously translated to another day, removed from the "current date" and its moods. Last night's deadly fear was what it was. The splintered shop window was what it was. The disorders beyond the Caucasus were what they were. My hand and her hip—they were. It was the warmth of earth colors from the path along the railroad to Versailles. A dream of the all-encompassing, all-absorbing book, long gone from the world, long dreamed to an end—was back again all of a sudden; or renewed? here in the daytime world, and needed only to be written down. A Mongoloid woman, or perhaps a saint, with a knapsack on her back ran across the pedestrian crossing in an ecstasy of terror. And that night there was only one customer in the bar of another small-town station; while the *patron* was drying glasses, the house cat was playing with a billiard ball between the tables, the jagged shadows of the plane-tree leaves were dancing over the dusty windowpane, and the urgent need arose to find a different word from "blinking" for the lights of a moving train seen through a curtain of foliage—as though the discovery of a single appropriate word could make this entire day successful in the sense that "all phenomena (or, in contemporary, secular terms: all forms) are light."

Then at last, in disregard of logic or timeliness, a third voice, obscure, dim of outline, stuttering-stammering, a storytelling voice that seemed to come from below, from the underbrush, from far away, butted into our essay on the successful day. —At last? Or unfortunately? To its detriment?

Fortunately or not, an "unfortunately" is in order, for a while at least; for in the following a relapse into hair-splitting cannot be avoided. Does Van Morrison's song tell of a successful day, or only of a happy one? Because in the present context a "successful day" was dangerous, fraught with obstacles, narrow escapes, ambushes, perils, tempests, comparable to the days of Odysseus on his homeward wanderings, a story of days that can end only in eating, drinking, reveling, and the "godlike bedding of a woman." But the dangers of my present day are neither the boulder from the giant's sling nor any of the other well-known perils; the dangerous part of my day is the day itself. Most likely this has always been the case, especially in epochs and parts of the world where wars and other catastrophes seemed far behind (how many diaries from how many so-called Golden Ages begin in the morning with resolutions for that one day and in the evening record their failure)—but when was such a day, yours or mine, ever seen before? And in an even more golden future mightn't its problem be even more timely and acute? At least for people like you and me, here and now in our halfway peaceful regions, the "specific demands of the day," quite apart from its duties, struggles, distractions—days as such, available days, each moment of which offers possibilities to be grasped at—have become a challenge, a potential friend, a potential enemy, a game of chance. But if such an adventure, or duel, or mere contest between you and the day, is to be withstood, conquered, made to bear fruit, it is essential that you receive no decisive help from any third factor, neither a piece of work nor the most delightful pastime, nor even from Van Morrison's bumpy ride; indeed, even such a distraction as "a short walk" would seem to be incompatible with a successful day—as though the day itself were the undertaking to be accomplished and brought home folded and packaged by me, preferably right here on the spot, while lying, sitting, standing, or at the most taking a few steps back and forth, doing nothing but looking and listening, or perhaps just breathing, but that involuntarily—with no effort on my part, as in every other segment of life on such a day—as though total involuntariness were prerequisite to this success. And would it thus give rise to a dance?

And now two fundamentally different versions of the individual's adventure with this day can be plotted. In the first he succeeds, the moment he wakes up, in casting off those dreams that are mere ballast that would encumber him on his course, and taking with him those that will form a counterweight to world events and the hap-

penings of his day; in the morning air the earth's conti-
nents merge; at the same time a crackling is heard in the
leaves of a bush in Tierra del Fuego; the alien light of
the afternoon, unbewitched from one moment to the next
through knowledge of a fata morgana emanating from
yourself; and from then on what's needed for success is
just to let night fall without losing your eyes for the dusk.
And then, though nothing has happened, you must have
it in you to go on interminably about your day. Ah, the
moment when at last there was nothing but the old man
in the blue apron in the front garden! And the opposite
version? It must be short—preferably something like this:
Paralyzed by the gray of dawn, a bundle of misery is cast
adrift; his ship, named *The Adventure of the Day*, capsizes
in the waters of the forenoon, so he never gets to know
the silence of midday, let alone the hours after that—and
ends up deep in the night at the exact same place from
which our hero should have started out at the crack of
dawn. To tell the truth, the words and images with which
to relate the failure of his day do not exist, except for
such worn-out allegories as we have just been using.

Thus it would seem that, before you can regard a day as
successful, every moment from waking to falling asleep
at night must count, or, more specifically, represent a trial
(or danger) faced. But aren't you struck by the fact that
for most other people a single moment counts as a successful day (and that there is something smug about your
conception so different from the prevailing view)? "When
I stood at the window in the dawning light, a little bird

darted by and let out a sound which seemed to be meant for me—that in itself was a successful day" (Narrator A). —"The day became successful at the moment when the phone—though you had no other plan than to go on reading the book—communicated to me the Wanderlust of your voice" (Narrator B). —"To be able to tell myself that the day is successful, I had no need of a particular moment—all I needed on waking was a mere breath, *un souffle*, or something of the sort" (a third narrator). And hasn't it occurred to you that as a rule the question of whether a day is to be successful has been decided before the day has properly begun?

Here at least we shall not count a single moment, however glorious, as a successful day. (We shall count only the whole day.) Nevertheless, the moments I have mentioned, especially the first moments of full consciousness after the night's sleep, may well provide the starting point for the Line of Beauty and Grace. And once the starting point for the day is set, let the day proceed point by point in a high arc. As I listen for a tone, the tonality of the whole day's journey reveals itself to me. The tone does not have to be a full sound, it can be indifferent, as often as not a mere noise; the essential is that I make myself all ears for it. Didn't the clicking of the buttons, when I stripped my shirt off the chair this morning, provide me with a kind of diapason for my day? And when yesterday morning, instead of reaching blindly and heedlessly for the first thing I needed, I did so carefully, with open eyes, didn't that supply me with the right rhythm for taking hold of things all the rest of the day? And mightn't the continual sensation of wind and water in the new morning—or, instead of "sensation," wouldn't it be preferable to say "awareness," or simply "feeling" in my eyes, my temples, and wrists—mightn't this sensation attune me to the coming elements of the day, prepare me to dissolve into them and let them work on me? (Answer reserved for the present.) Such a successful moment: Viaticum? Impulse? Nourishment with breath as spirit for the rest of this one day; for such a moment gives strength, and in telling about the next moment one might, drawing on another literal translation of "moment" again from a Pauline epistle, begin with "And with one casting of the eye . . .": With one casting of the eye the sky turned blue, and with the next casting of the eye the green of the grass became a greening, and . . . Who has ever experienced a successful day? But who has ever experienced a successful day? Not to mention the difficulty of tracing the curve of that line!

The clouds of the still invisible dog's breath came puffing through the cracks in the fence. The few remaining leaves on the trees trembled in the foggy wind. The forest began just behind the village railroad station. Two men were washing the telephone booth; the one outside was white, the one inside was black.

And if I fail to seize a moment of this kind, does it mean that my whole day has failed? If this last apple, instead of being carefully picked, were torn blindly from the branch—would all the preceding consonances between the day and me be nullified? If I were insensitive to the glance of a child, evaded the beggar's glance, were unable to face the glance of that woman (or even of that drunk) —would that mean a break in my rhythm, a fall from my day? And would it be impossible to make a fresh start that same day? Would that day's failure be irrevocable? With the consequence that for me the daylight would not only diminish as it does for most other people, but also, and this is where the danger lies, that brightness of form might degenerate into the hell of formlessness? Thus, for example, if the musical clicking of the buttons against the wood were repeated on such an unsuccessful day, I should be condemned to hear it as noise. Or if in a moment of carelessness I were to reach out "blindly" for a glass and drop it, causing it to shatter into smithereens, wouldn't that be a catastrophe and far more than a mere mishap, though of course everyone else in the room would deny it: —the incursion of death into the current day? And would I be condemned—and rightly so—as the most presumptuous of beings, because in aspiring to live a successful day I had wanted to be like a god? For the idea of such a day—to move onward and ever onward on the same level while carrying light—is, after all, a project fit only for our ill-fated Lucifer. Does this mean that my attempt at a successful day is in danger of degenerating at any moment into a story of murder and mayhem, of running amok, devastation, annihilation, and suicide?

·   ·   ·

You are confusing a successful day with a perfect day. (No need to say anything about the latter or its god.) At the end of a thoroughly imperfect day, you might cry out in spite of yourself: "A successful day!" Conceivable, too, is a day during which you have been painfully aware of unsuccessful moments, and yet at the end of which you report at length to your friends on "a striking success." Your leaving the book which, as you sensed in reading the first line, started the day off right, in the train, needn't mean that you've lost your fight with the angel of the day; even if you never find the book again, your reading that began so full of promise may well continue in a different manner—perhaps more freely, more spontaneously. The success of my days seems to depend on how I evaluate (another ugly word, but the brooding writer finds no better—"appraise"? "estimate"?) deviations from the line, my own as well as those imposed by Madame World. The success of our "successful day" expedition seems to presuppose a certain indulgence toward myself, my nature, my incorrigibilities, as well as an insight into the hazards of daily life even under favorable circumstances: the insidiousness of objects, evil eye, that one word spoken at the wrong moment (even if only overheard by someone in a crowd). Thus in my undertaking, everything hinges on the handicap I allow myself. How much mucking around, how much carelessness or absentmindedness I tolerate in myself. How much incomprehension, impatience, unfairness, how much clumsiness, how many heartless remarks, spoken without thinking (or not even spoken), how many newspaper headlines, or advertisements that catch my eye or ear, how many stitches in my side will it take before I lose my openness to the shimmering that corresponds to the episodic greening and blueing of grass and sky, and the occasional "graying" of stone, signifying that on a certain day the "coming of day" carries over to me and to space. I am too hard on myself, not indifferent enough about my mishaps with things, too full of demands on the times, too convinced that everything is going to the dogs: I have no standard for the success of a day. Indeed, what with myself and the kind of things that happen regularly or irregularly, the situation would seem to call for a special kind of irony—the affectionate kind—and of humor, of the sort named after the gallows. Who has ever experienced a successful day?

His day began promisingly. A few lance-shaped pencils lay on the windowsill along with a handful of oval hazelnuts. Even the numbers of both sets of objects contributed to his sense of well-being. He had dreamed about a child lying on the bare floor in a bare room, who said when he bent down to him: "You're a good father." On the street the postman whistled as he did every morning. The old woman in the house next door was already closing her dormer window for the rest of the day. The sand in the columns of trucks en route to the building site was as yellow as the drifting sand that made up the hills of the region. By letting the water in the hollow of his hand act on his face, he had gained awareness not only of the water in the village here but also of the "water of Ioannia on the far slope of the Pindus," of the "water of Bitola in Macedonia," of the water that morning in Santander, where the rain seemed to be pelting down, but when he went out proved to be so fine a curtain that he hardly got wet when passing through it. With the sound of a turning book page in his ears, he heard from far beyond the gardens the clanking of the local train slowing down in the station and at the same time, amid the squawking of the crows and the whining of the magpies, the lone cheeping of a sparrow. Then he looked up, never before had he seen the bare, solitary tree high up on the edge of the wooded hill, through whose branches as they shifted in the wind the brightness of the plateau shone down into the house, while on the table at which he sat reading, the letter S, sewn into the tablecloth, revealed a picture of an apple and of a smooth, black, rounded stone. When he looked up again—"work can wait, I can wait, it and I, we can both wait"—the day was literally whirring, and he noticed now, without having looked for the words, he was thinking to himself: "Sacred world!" He went out into the forest to chop wood for a fire in the fireplace, which it seemed to him would be better suited to such a day rather than to the evening. As he was sawing the thick, tough tree, the blade stuck, breaking his rhythm; he tugged violently, but it refused to budge; he could only give up, pull—or better, "wrench" the saw out—and start in a different place. The whole comedy repeated itself— the blade stuck in the heartwood, he pushed and shook until he had almost reached the point of no return . . . and then with stunning force the log, more mangled than sawed, fell on the foot of the would-be hero of the day.

Finally, after a first flaring and a subdued hissing, his fire collapsed, and he cursed the holy day in the exact same words for which his rustic grandfather had been known throughout the village: Shut up, blasted birds, beat it, sun. Later, it sufficed for his pencil point to break, and not only the day, but the future as well, was compromised. By the time he realized that these very mishaps might have made something of the day, it had long since become a different day. If he had observed it with care, he would have recognized that this vain attempt to light a fire— hadn't the smothering and blackening of the flame represented a mysterious moment of community?—was the quintessence of all futilities, and not only those of a personal nature. If he had recognized this, he would have stopped trying and exercised patience. And similarly, the blow of the log on his toes had given him something more than pain. It had also touched something else in him, at the same place; something like the friendly muzzle of an animal. And that again was an image—an image in which all the logs from his childhood down to the present moment united to fall—or rather, to roll, bounce, dance, or rain down on all his different shoes, socks, and variously sized child or adult feet; for that other contact was so miraculously gentle that if he had merely taken note of it for a moment he would have been all amazement. And similarly, as he realized later on when he looked back at a distance, his setbacks while sawing wood provided him with a complete parable, or fable?, for the success of his day. The main thing was to begin with a jolt and find the right starting point for the saw's teeth, a groove in which the saw could continue to function. After that, the sawing took on a rhythm. For a time it went easily and gave him pleasure; one thing led to another; sawdust sprayed from both sides, the tiny leaves of the nearby box tree curled, the crackling of the foliage caught in it mingled with the squeaking of the saw; the rumble of a garbage can was followed by the droning of a jet plane high in the sky. And then, gradually as a rule and, provided he kept his mind on what he was doing, perceptible in advance, the saw entered into a different layer of the wood. Here it became necessary to change his rhythm— to slow down, but that was the risky part of it—to do so without halting or skipping a beat; even when the rhythm changed, the general sawing movement had to maintain its regularity; otherwise, the saw would be sure to stick. Then, if at all possible, one had to pull it out and reapply it, preferably, as the fable taught, not in the same place or in one too close to it, but in a totally different place, because . . . If the change of place was successful at the second try, and the sawing was finally successful in the lower half of the tree trunk—long after the exhilarated sawyer had lost sight of the saw's teeth—already he was elsewhere in his thoughts, making plans for the evening or sawing a human enemy in two instead of the tree— then a new danger threatened, if not a forking branch he had overlooked, then (usually no more than a finger's breadth from the point where the piece of wood, having been cut through that far, would fall of its own accord) that narrow but extremely tough layer in which steel would strike against stone, nail, and bone all in one, and just before the finale, so to speak, the undertaking would come to grief. For a brief moment, music to the ears of a stranger but to the sawyer himself caterwauling—and that was the end of it. And yet he had been so close to success that sawing for its own sake, just being with the wood, its roundness, its smell, its grain, just traversing the material, while studying its special characteristics and resistances, became the ideal embodiment of his dream of disinterested pleasure. And likewise the breaking pencil point . . . and so forth and so on, all day. Thus, he reflected later, in an attempt at a successful day, everything, at least in moments of misfortune, of pain, of failure, when things were going wrong—the essential was to summon up the presence of mind needed for a different variety of this moment and thus to transform it, by a liberating act of awareness or reflection, whereby the day—as though this were the prerequisite for its success—would acquire its élan and its wings.

You make it sound as though your successful day were child's play.

No answer.

By then it was noon. The night's hoarfrost had thawed even in the shaded corners of the garden, and as the bowed, stiff blades of grass straightened up, a soft breeze blew through them. A stillness arose, became a picture when he walked in the sunlight on the untraveled noon-day road, with those pairs of varicolored butterflies which, emerging unexpectedly out of the void, seemed to be moving backward and came so close to the wayfarer that he seemed to feel in his outer ears the vibration of their wings, which instantly communicated itself to his steps. For the first time he heard, in the interior of the almost uninhabited house, the midday bells of the village church mingling with those of the next village (which, as usual in this part of the country, began without transition or interval, on the other side of the street) ring out with a palpable message: a call in all directions to all isolated beings. The city of Paris lay deep at the bottom of a bowl, surrounded by stony desert mountains, and in the soundless dusk the fervid calls of the muezzins poured down upon it from every peak and slope round about. Involuntarily he looked up from the line he was reading and went out with the cat, crossing the garden in a long, curving diagonal; it passed through his mind how long ago another cat had announced the onset of rain by galloping to shelter under the overhanging roof the moment the first drop from the distant horizon fell on its fur. He looked around, noted, as he had done for weeks, how the garden's last fruit, one enormous pear, still hung on the otherwise empty tree, and hefted it for a moment in the hollow of his hand, while across the street, in the neighboring village, a black-haired Chinese girl carrying a varicolored back satchel kept stroking a blue-eyed Alaskan dog through the fence (though he could not hear it, the dog's whimpering was all the more prolonged in his imagination), and a little farther on, in the gap between the houses at the distant junction of two streets, the sun's

reflection on a passing train lit up the grass of the embankment for a moment, the length as it were of a word,
a monosyllable, during which he glimpsed an empty seat
in one compartment, slashed with a knife and mended
with fairytale care, cross-stitch after cross-stitch in the stiff
plastic fabric, and he felt himself gripped by the faraway
hand that was pulling the thread tight. Thus his forehead
grazed his dead; he watched them just as they watched
him, he who was doing nothing but sitting there, sym-
pathetically, not at all as in their lifetime. What more was
there to do, to discover, to recognize, to discover in a day?
Behold: no king of eternity, no king of life (and if so only
a "secret" one)— No, here stands the king of the day!
The only odd part of it was that at this point a trifle
sufficed to topple him from his imperious throne. At the
sight of the passerby who came sauntering out of the side
street, with his coat over his arm, stopped, patted his
pockets, and quickly turned back, my sympathy turned
to desperation. Stop! But once in ecstasy I could no longer
find the way back into myself: There, the blackbird's
yellow bill. And, at the end of the avenue, the brownish
edge of the one mallow still in bloom. And that leaf—
tugging at an invisible thread as it falls, and apparently
rising back into the sun—it looks like a bright-colored
kite. And the horizon, black with a swarm of monumental, meaningless words! Stop! Leave me in peace! (To
him ecstasy meant panic.) But enough! Stop! —No more
reading, gazing, being-in-the-picture, no more day—this
couldn't go on. What now? And unexpectedly, after the
procession of leaping forms and ecstatic colors, long before

nightfall, death barred the passage through this day. At one stroke, its sting punctured the whole extravaganza. After that, could anything be more crackbrained than the idea of a successful day? Mustn't his essay on it start all over again, with a radically new attitude, that of gallows humor? Is it impossible to lay down a line for the success of a day, not even a labyrinthine line? But must one not infer that this constant starting the essay from scratch is itself a possibility, the possibility specific to the project? The essay must be. Quite possibly the day (the object named "day") had now become my mortal enemy, an enemy that cannot be transformed into a helpful living-and-traveling companion, a luminous model, a lasting fragrance, quite possibly the "successful day" project is diabolical, an invention of the devil, the disrupter, a veil dance with nothing behind it, a maddening tongue play, followed directly by a devouring, a road pointer which, if you follow it, closes into a noose; that may be, but I fail to see why, in view of all the failures I have met with in my quest for a successful day, I am still unable to *say* that the idea of a successful day is a snare and a delusion, and consequently that cannot be the case. I can say, however, that the idea is indeed an idea, for I didn't think it up or get it from my reading; it came to me in a time of distress, and it came with a power which for me has always carried credibility—the power of the imagination. Imagination is my faith, the idea of a successful day was conceived in its most ardent moment, and after each one of my countless shipwrecks, on the following morning (or afternoon) it lit the way for me anew, just as in Mörike's poem a rose "vorleuchtet" (shone before), and I was able with its help to make a fresh start. The success of the day was something that had to be attempted—even if in the end the fruit turned out to be hollow or dry: thus this vain labor of love was superfluous at least for the foreseeable future, and then the road would be open for something different. And another dependable insight was that a "nothing" day (a day marked not even by changing lights, a day without wind or weather) gave promise of the utmost richness. Nothing was, and again there was nothing, and again there was nothing. And what did this nothing and again nothing do? It signified. More was possible with nothing but the day, far far more both for you and for me. And that was the crux: the main thing was to let the nothing fructify from morning to night (or even midnight). And I repeat: the day was light. The day is light.

The blackness of the nameless pond in the woods. Snow clouds above the Île de France horizon. The smell of pencils. The ginkgo leaf on the boulder in the garden of La Pagode cinema. The carpet in the topmost window of the Vélizy railroad station. A school, a pair of children's glasses, a book, a hand. The whirring in my temples. For the first time this winter, the powerful cracking of the ice under the soles of my shoes. In the railroad underpass, he acquired eyes for the substance of light. Reading in a crouch, close to the grass. While I was breaking off leaves, suddenly a whiff in my nostrils resembling the essence of the declining year. The word for the sound of the train pulling into the station had to be "thumping," not "clank-ing." And the last leaf falling from the tree didn't "crackle," it "clicked." And a stranger involuntarily ex-changed greetings with him. And again the old woman hauled her pushcart to the weekly village market. And the usual disorientation of a foreign car driver in this out-of-the-way place. And then in the forest, the greening of the path where he used to take a walk with his father whenever there was something to talk over, a path that even had a name in his language, *zelena pot*, "the green path." And then in the bar near the church of the next village, the pensioner, whose grandfather's watch chain extended in a curved line from his belly to his trouser pocket. And for once he overlooked the evil eye cast by one of the old inhabitants. And the proverbial "Thanks [instead of dis-gruntlement] for your trouble"; for once the transfor-mation was successful. But why then in the middle of the enjoyable afternoon, fear of the rest of the day, of nothing but the day? As though there were no getting through the coming hours ("This day will be the end of me")—no way out. The ladder leaning against the early-winter tree. So what? The blue of the flowers deep in the grass of the railroad embankment—so what? Paralysis, con-sternation, a kind of horror, and the serene silence shat-tered by more and more speechlessness. Eden is burning. And, on the other hand, it becomes evident that there is no formula for the success of a day. "O morning!" The exclamation doesn't work. No more reading, no more day? No more possession of words? No more day? And such muteness excludes prayer, all but such impossible

prayers as "Morning me," "Early me," "Begin me again."
Who knows whether certain mysterious suicides were the
secret consequences of such a quest for the successful day,
begun energetically on the so-called ideal line. But, on
the other hand, doesn't my failure to stand up to the day
tell me something? That my internal order is wrong?
That I'm not made for a whole day? That I shouldn't
look for morning at nightfall? Or perhaps I should?

And he made it start again. The day when the idea of
the successful day had come to live in him on the tangent
of the suburban train high above gigantic Paris—how
had it been as a whole? What was before that flare-up?
What came after it? ("*Ausculta, o filii*, listen, my son,"
said the angel in the church on Lake Constance, where
the chalky vein had copied Hogarth's Line of Beauty and
Grace for him on the black stone.) —What had gone
before, he remembered, was a nightmarish night spent
on a mattress in an otherwise totally deserted house in a
southern suburb of Paris. This dream had consisted of
nothing, or so it had seemed, but a night-long motionless
image, in which, amid unchanging twilight and soundless
air, he was exposed to the elements on a bare, towering
cliff, alone for the rest of his life. And only one thing
happened, but that happened perpetually, heartbeat after
heartbeat, utter forlornness—the planet was congealed,
but in his heart tempestuous fever. When he finally awoke,
it was as though his night-long fever had consumed his
forlornness—for a time at least. Over the half-parched
garden the sky was blue, for the first time in a long while.

He helped himself out of his feeling of dizziness with a dance step, "the dizzy man's dance." The world went green before his eyes, that was the cypresses along the garden wall. Under the sign of grief and of this green he began his day. What would I be without a garden? he thought. I never want to be without a garden again. And still there was pain in his breast, a dragon devouring him. Sparrows landed in the bushes, once again the birds of the right moment. I saw a ladder and wanted to climb it. A mason's straight edge was floating in the gutter, and farther down the street the young postwoman was pushing her bicycle with the yellow saddlebags. Instead of "propriété privée, défense d'entrer," he read ". . . défense d'aimer." It was late morning, and as he walked he let the quietness of the place blow through his parted fingers. Temples, inflated sails. He was supposed that day to finish an article on translation, and at last he had an image for that sort of activity: "The translator felt himself gently taken by the elbow." Work or love? Get to work, that's the way to rediscover love. The man behind the counter in the North African bar was just starting up: "O rage! O désespoir . . ." and a woman on her way in remarked "It doesn't smell of couscous here. It smells of ragout, that's because the sun is back again—merci pour le soleil." Give me the day, give me to the day. After a long bus ride through the southern and then the western suburbs and a hike through the forests of Clamart and Meudon, he sat down at a table in the open beside a pond, finished his piece about translation, an activity which he abjured in his last sentence: "Not the confident, lowered glance at the existing book, but an eye-level glance into the uncertain!" The wild strawberries at the edge of the path seemed to look on and blush. "The wind took him over." He thought of the raven which bellowed "like a bazooka" into his dream of forlornness. By the pond of the next forest he ate a sandwich on the terrace of the fishermen's bar. A fine rain was falling in spirals, as though enjoying itself. And then, in the middle of the afternoon, that train ride circling around above Paris, first eastward, then northward in an arc, then back in an eastward arc—so that in a single day he had almost circled the entire metropolis—during which the idea of the successful day recurred, no, "recurred" was not the right word, it should have been "was transformed": during which the idea of the successful day was transformed from a "life idea" to a "writing idea." His heart, which still ached from his nightmare, expanded when he saw the "Heights of the Seine" at his feet. (Suddenly he understood the name of the department, Les Hauts-de-Seine.) Illusion? No. The true element of life. And then what? Now, half a year later, in the late autumn, he remembered how after the excessively bright life of the "casting of the eye," he had positively welcomed the dark, underground stretch near La Défense. Exhilarated, he let himself be jostled by the after-work crowd in the hall of the Gare Saint-Lazare, which in French is known as the Hall of the Lost Steps. At the American Express Company near the Opéra he provided himself with as much cash as possible after waiting in a long line with rare, and in his own opinion rather alarming, patience. Amazed at the size and emptiness of the toilets, he stayed there longer than necessary, looking around, as though there were something to be discovered in such a place. One of a crowd, he stood watching television in a bar on the rue Saint-Denis; a World Cup soccer match was on, and to this day he remembers his annoyance at not having quite succeeded in repressing all side glances at the streetwalkers who were overflowing from every doorway and back court of that street—as though ability to overlook were a part of such a day. And then what? He seemed to have lost consciousness of everything else, except for a moment later in the evening when he sat with a child on his lap at a kind of school desk, putting the finishing touches to his sketch about translation—in his memory, a strange picture of juggling with two hands—and for some time late at night when in a garden café I found myself unintentionally exchanging stories with the man sitting across from you—which had the effect of the gentlest possible way of breaking you open and sharing you with myself. Then as now the day seemed marked by that gigantic S-curve of the railroad line, which can be seen only in bird's-eye view, but can be felt deep down inside to be the most beautiful of all meanders, parallel to that of the Seine below but swinging much wider, rediscovered a month later in a quiet corner of the Tate Gallery in the furrow in Hogarth's palette, and yet another month later in the white vein in the stone found on the shore of the stormy, autumnal Lake Constance, at the present moment running in the same direction as the pencils here on my table: that is the enduring outline of the day. And its color is chiaroscuro.

And its adjective, like that of the idea which it gave me, is, as it should be, "fantastic," and its noun, after my solitary night of peril, the word "with."

So your idea of writing an essay about a successful day was itself a successful day?

That was before the summer. Over the garden the swallows were flying "so high!" I shared a young woman's pleasure in smoothing out the curved brim of a straw hat; the Pentecost fête was lively in the night wind of our village, the cherry tree stood fruit-red beside the railroad tracks, the workaday garden came to be called the Garden of the Step Taken—and now it was winter, as, for example, it revealed itself on the railroad curve repeated yesterday for my reassurance as I could see by the handrail and the gray flowering of the clumps of wild grapes against the misty network of the Eiffel Tower, the snowberries whishing past the distant towers of La Défense, the acacia thorn jerking past the barely discernible hazy whiteness of the domes of Sacré-Coeur.

Once again: In the light of all this, was that a successful day?

No answer.

I think no, thanks to my imagination, I know it was. How much more could be done with that day, with nothing but that day. And now its momentum is in my life,

in your life, in our epoch. ("We lost our momentum,"
said the captain of a baseball team, which had been about
to win the game.) The day is in my power, for my time.
If I don't give the day a try now, then I've missed my
chance of enduring; more and more often, I realize, all
the while growing angrier at myself, how as time goes
on more and more moments speak to me and how I
understand, and above all appreciate, less and less of what
they say. I must repeat, I am furious with myself, over
my inability to maintain the morning light on the horizon,
which just now made me look up and come to rest (*into*
rest, we read in the Pauline epistle), so that, when I start
reading, the blue of the heather still occupies the middle
ground, a few pages farther on it is a vague spot in the
Nowhere, and by the onset of dusk the motionless form
of the blackbird in the bush is still "the outline of Evening
Island after a day on the open sea," and a tick of the
watch later is nothing more—meaningless, forgotten, betrayed. Yes, that's how it is: more and more as the years
go by—the richer the moments seem to me, the louder
they denounce me to high heaven—I see myself as a
traitor to my day, day after day, forgetful of the day,
forgetful of the world. Again and again I resolve to remain
faithful to the day, with the help, led "by the hand"
("maintenant," hand-holding, that's your word for "now")
of those moments. I would like to hold them, think about
them, preserve them, and day after day, no sooner have
I turned away from them than they literally "fall" from
my hands, as though to punish me for my infidelity, for,
it can't be denied, I had turned away from them. Fewer

and fewer of the increasingly frequent significant moments of the day *ripen*, yes, that's the word, ripen anything
for me. The moment of the children's voices this morning
in the lane ripened nothing; now in the afternoon, with
clouds drifting eastward, it produces no aftereffect—
though at the time they seemed to rejuvenate the wintry
forest . . . Should that be taken to mean that the time for
my essay on the successful day is past? Have I let the
moment slip by? Should I have gotten up earlier? And
rather than an essay, mightn't the psalm form—a sup-
plication presumed in advance to be in vain—have been
more conducive to the idea of such a day? Day, let everything in you ripen something for me. Ripen the ticking
of the lanceolate willow leaves as they fall through the
air, the left-handed ticket agent deep in his book, who
once again makes me wait for my ticket, the sun on the
door handle. Ripen me. I've become my own enemy, I
destroy the light of my day, destroy my love, destroy
my book. The more often individual moments resound
as pure vowels—"vowel" is another word for such a
moment—the more seldom I find the consonant to go
with it, to carry me through the day. The glow at the
end of the sandy path to the nameless pond: Ah! but a
moment later it has faded, as though it had never been.
Divine Being, or "Thou, the more-than-I" that once spoke
through the Prophets and later on "through the Son,"
dost thou also speak in the present, purely through the
day? And why am I unable to hold, grasp, pass on what
thus speaks through the day, and, I believe, or rather,
thanks to my imagination, know, starts speaking anew at

every moment? "He who is and who was and who will be": why can what once was said of "the god" not be said of my present day?

On a successful day—attempt at a chronicle of this day —globules of dew on a raven feather. As usual, the old woman, though perhaps not the same one as yesterday, stood around in the newspaper shop long after completing her purchase, and spoke her mind. The ladder in the garden—embodiment of his need to get out of himself —had seven rungs. The sand in the trucks moving through the village was the same color as the façade of Saint-Germain-des-Près. The chin of a young girl in the library touched her neck. A tin bucket took its shape. A mailbox turned yellow. The market woman wrote the bill on the palm of her hand. On a successful day it happens that a cigarette butt rolls in the gutter, that a cup smokes on a tree stump, and that a row of seats within the dark church is bright in the sunshine. It happens that the few men in the café, even the loudmouth, keep silent together for a long moment, and that the stranger to the village keeps silent with them. It happens that my sharpened hearing for my work also opens me up to the sounds in the house. It happens that one of your eyes is smaller than the other, that the blackbird hops under the bush, and that when the lower branches rise I think "updraft." Finally, it even happens that nothing happens. On the successful day, a habit will be discontinued, an opinion vanish, and I shall be surprised by him, by you, by myself. And along with "with," a second word form will dominate; namely, "and." In the house I shall discover a corner that has hitherto been overlooked, where "someone could live!" As I turn into a side street, "Where am I? I've never been here before" will be a sensational moment; when I see the light-dark space in a hedge, the "New-World explorer" feeling will set in, and when I walk a little farther than usual and look back, a cry of "I never saw that before" will escape me. Your repose, as sometimes happens in children, will also be amazement. On the successful day, I shall simply have been its medium, simply have gone along with the day, let the sun shine on me, the wind blow on me, the rain rain on me, my verb will have been "let." In the course of the day, your inwardness will become as varied as the outside world, and by the end of the day you will have translated Odysseus' epithet, "the much-buffeted," to yourself as "the many-sided," and that many-sidedness will have made you dance inwardly. On a successful day, the hero would have been able to "laugh" at his mishaps (or would at least have started to laugh at the third mishap). He would have been in the company of forms—if only of the various leaves on the ground. His I-day would have opened out into a world-day. Every place would have acquired its moment, and he would have been able to say: "This is it." He would have arrived at an understanding with mortality. ("Never has death spoiled the sport of the day.") His epithet for everything would have been an unchanging "In view of": In view of you, in view of a rose, in view of the asphalt, and matter, or "corporeity"?, would have cried out to him, time and again for creation. He would have put on a show of good cheer and cheerfully done nothing, and from time to time a weight on his back would have kept him warm. For a moment, for a "casting of the eye," the time of a word, he would suddenly have become you. And at the end of the day he would have called out for a book—something more than a mere chronicle: "The fairy tale of the successful day." And at the very end, he would have gloriously forgotten that the day was supposed to be successful . . .

Have you ever experienced a successful day? Everyone I know has experienced one; most people have actually had many. One was satisfied if the day hadn't been too long. Another said something like: "Standing on the bridge, with the sky over me. In the morning, laughed with the children. Just looking, nothing special. There's happiness in looking." And in the opinion of a third, simply the village street through which he had just passed—with the raindrops dripping from the enormous key of the locksmith's sign, with the bamboo shoots cooking in somebody's front garden, with the three bowls on a kitchen windowsill containing tangerines, grapes, and peeled potatoes, with the taxi parked as usual outside the driver's house—was in itself a "successful day." The priest, whose pet word was "longing," considered a day when he heard a friendly voice successful. And hadn't he himself, who longed time and again for an hour in which nothing had happened, except that a bird turned about on a branch, that a white ball lay at the bottom of a bush, and that schoolchildren were sunning themselves on the station platform, thought in spite of himself: Has this been the whole day? And often in the evening, when he called the events of the past day to mind—yes, it was a kind of "calling"—didn't the things or places of a mere moment occur to him as names for it. "That was the day when the man with the baby carriage went zigzagging through the piles of leaves." "That was the day when the gardener's banknotes were mixed with grass and leaves." "That was the day when the café was empty when the refrigerator rumbled and the light went out . . ." So why not content ourselves with a single successful hour? Why not simply call the moment a day?

Ungaretti's poem "I illuminate myself with the immeasurable" is entitled "Morning." Couldn't those two lines just as well be about the "afternoon"? Were a fulfilled moment or a fulfilled hour really enough to make you stop asking if you had failed again that day? No use attempting a successful day—why not content ourselves with a "not entirely unsuccessful one"? And if your successful day existed, wasn't your fantasy, however richly and wonderfully it whirred, accompanied by a strange fear of something like an alien planet, and didn't your usual unsuccessful day appear to you as part of the planet earth, as a kind of—possibly detested—home? As though nothing here below could succeed; except perhaps in grace? in mercy? in grace *and* mercy—if nowadays that didn't imply something improper, undeserved, perhaps even accomplished at someone else's expense? Why now does "successful day" remind me of my dead grandfather, who in his last days did nothing but scratch the wall of his room with his fingernails, lower down from hour to hour. In view of all the general failure and loss, what does a single success amount to?

Not nothing.

The day of which I can say it was "a day," and the day when I was only passing the time. At the crack of dawn. How have people handled their days up to now? How is it that in old stories we often find "Many days were fulfilled," in place of "Many days passed"? Traitor to the day: my own heart. It drives me out of the day, it beats, it hammers me out of it, hunter and hunted in one. Be still! No more secret thoughts. Leaves in my garden shoes. Out of the cage of revolving thought. Be still. Bend down under the apple tree. Go into a crouch. The crouching reader. At knee height, things coalesce to form an environment. And he prepares for the daily injury. Spreads his toes. "The seven days of the garden." That's what the unwritten sequel to *Don Quixote* should be called. To be in the garden, to be on earth. The rate of the earth's rotation is irregular, that's why the days are of unequal length, especially in view of the mountain ranges' resistance to the wind. The success of the day and passivity. Passivity as action. He let the fog drift outside the window; he let the grass blow behind the house. Letting the sun shine on one was an activity; now I'm going to let my forehead be warmed, now my eyeballs, now my knees— and now it's time for teddy-bear warmth between my shoulder blades. The sunflower head does nothing but follow the sun. Compare the successful day with Job's day. Instead of "value the moment," it should be "heed" the moment. The course of the day—thanks precisely to its rough spots, if taken to heart—is in itself a kind of transubstantiation—more than anything else, it can tell me *what I am.* Pause in your endless restlessness, and you will find rest in your flight. And by resting in his flight, he began to hear. Hearing, I am at my peak. Thanks to my keen hearing, I can hear the whirring of a sparrow's wing through the noise. When a leaf falls on the line of the distant horizon, I hear it deep inside me as a ringing. Listening as a safecracker with his jimmy listens for the clicking of the gears. Slowed by flight, the blackbird's hop-skip-jump over the hedge is humming a tune for me. Just as some people hum when reading a book. (But the most you can expect of a newspaper reader is a whistling between the teeth.) "Seeing you are dull of hearing," stormed the zealot in one of his epistles, and in another: "Stop disputing over mere words, it does no good and only bedevils those who listen." A pure tone. If only I could produce a pure tone once for a whole day. Perhaps more important than hearing is pure presence—Picasso's last wife, for example, is said to have done nothing, just to have been present in his studio. A successful day, a hard day. Suddenly, as I was raking the garden leaves, a rooster's foot gleamed candlelight yellow from out of the pile of brownish leaves. Colors darken, form brightens. In the shady corner, where the ground is still frozen hard, my footsteps sound as they did that day in the rushes.

When I look up, the sky is a vault. What did "snow cloud" mean? Rich whiteness with a blue cast. Cracking hazelnuts in the palm of my hand, three of them. In Greek there used to be a word for "I am," which was simply a long-drawn-out "O"; it occurred in such sentences as "While I am in the world, I am the light of the world." And the word for what just passed through the cypress tree was: "lightwave." Look and keep looking with the eyes of the right word. And it began to snow. It is snowing. Il neige. To be silent. There was silence. He was silent in the sign of the dead. One should not say: "He (she) blessed the temporal world" (He [she] passed away) but: "He, she, the dead, bless the temporal world for me, provided I leave them alone." And at the same time wanting to stammer: he wanted to stammer. In the suburbs everything is supposedly so "individual" (a suburbanite speaking). The one-legged stance of the garbage collector at the back of his truck. The bumps placed on the roads at regular intervals were called "decelerators." A single day may not have been sufficiently far-reaching as a model; perhaps it was a model only to itself—which gave pleasure? During the lunch break I help the roofers carry slats down from the ridge. Shouldn't I have stayed home all day, doing nothing but "dwelling"? Bring about a successful day by pure dwelling? To dwell, to sit, to look up, to excel in uselessness. What did you do today? I heard. What did you hear? Oh, the house. Ah, beneath the tent of my book. But why are you going out now, instead of staying in the house, where you were in your place with your book? Because what I've read—I want to digest it out of doors. And look at the corner of the house, which is called "Travels": a small suitcase, a dictionary, hiking shoes. The ringing of bells in the belfry of the village church: the pitch is just right for this noon hour, and up here in the dark dormer window all that can be seen of them is a whirring as of bicycle spokes. Deep within the earth, there are occasional tremors, the so-called slow tremors, and for a while, so it is said, the planet reverberates with them: "the bell movement," the ringing of the earth. The silhouettes of a man and a child with a back satchel sway in the railroad underpass, as if the man were riding on a donkey. According to Goethe, life is short but the day is long, and I seem to remember Marilyn Monroe singing a song that went: "One day too long, one life too short . . . " and another: "Morning becomes evening under my body." Let the quick ellipse described by the last of the leaves of the plane tree in falling provide the line for the ending of my attempted successful day—Abbreviation! Hogarth's Line of Beauty is not actually engraved in the palette; it is stretched over it like a curved rope or a whiplash. The successful day and succinctness. (And, alongside it, the desire to postpone the end—as though I, I in particular, could learn more from my essay with each passing day.) The successful day and joyful expectation. The successful day and the discoverer's aberrations. Morning a still life—afternoon a muddle: a mere pseudolaw? Don't let yourself be ruled by these daily pseudolaws. And once again St. Paul. For him "the day" is the Day of Judgment—and for you? The day of measurement; it will not judge, but measure you; you are its people. Who here is talking to whom? I'm talking to myself. The dead silence of the afternoon. Nevertheless, the sound of children running, heard through the wind. And high up there the flower heads of the plane trees are still dangling: "his (her) heart is in it" (from the French). And at any moment, in the rustling of the withered dwarf oaks, now, for instance, I become you. What would we be without that rustling? And what word goes with it? The (toneless) yes. Stay with us, rustling. Keep pace with the day—speak in cadence with the day (homology). What became of that day on the curve high above all Paris, between Saint-Cloud and Suresnes, not far from the Val d'Or station. It hung in the balance. The bright-dark shimmer that day when the swallows veered in the summer sky, and the black-white-blue moment now: the magpies and the winter sky. The S-line again, a few days ago, on the shoulder, neck, and throat of John the Evangelist at the Last Supper over the portal of Saint-Germain-des-Près, his whole trunk lies there on the table next to the Lord Jesus—for, like the other stone figures, he had been beheaded by the Revolution. The successful day and again history's glorious forgetfulness: instead, the endless lozenge pattern of human eyes—on the streets, in the corridors of the Métro, in the trains. The gray of the asphalt, the blue of the evening sky. The shakiness of my day, the solid and enduring? Set your footprint upon the snow of the station platform beside the print of a bird's foot. A hard day once began to teeter when a single raindrop struck my inner ear. The shoe brush on the

wooden stairs at sunset. A child writing its name for the
first time. Keep going until the first star. Van Morrison
in his song doesn't sing about "fishing in the mountains,"
but "out all day," about bird watching. He lets his tongue
sing, and barely begun, his song is at an end. The moment
of the mud-spattered forester's car in the row of clean
cars. The doors of the forest open with a creak. Revolving
door of a successful day: in it, things as well as people
flare up as *beings*. The successful day and the will to divide
it. Constant, wild obligation to be fair. Oh, hard day!
Successful? Or "saved"? Unexpectedly, still in the dark,
the thrust of joy in carrying on. Yes, a modified word—
a proof correction that stands for the day: "thrust" instead
of your usual "jolt." Stop on your night walk: the path
is brightening—for once you can say "my path"—and
increasing awareness of secrecy, "behold, she comes with
the clouds," comes with the wind. Triad of the screech
owl. Blue moment of the boat in one woodland pond,
black moment of the boat in the next pond. For the first
time in this suburb, behind the Heights of the Seine that
hide the lights of Paris, caught sight of Orion high in the
winter night, behind it parallel columns of smoke from
factory chimneys, and under it the five stone steps, leading
up to a door in a wall, and Ingrid Bergman in *Stromboli*,
who collapses after an almost fatal night on the black,
rocky slopes of the volcano, revives at sunrise, and can't
get over her amazement. "How beautiful! What beauty!"
In the 171 night bus a lone passenger, standing. The
burned-out telephone booth. Collision between two cars
at the Pointe de Chaville: from one of them leaps a man

with a pistol. Glaring television lights in the front windows of the Avenue Roger Salengro, the house numbers on which go up to over 2000. The thunder of the bombers taking off from the military airfield in Villacoublay, just beyond the wooded hills, more frequently from day to day with the approach of war.

"But now you're losing the line completely. Go home to your book, to writing and reading. To the original texts, in which for example it is said: 'Let the word resound, stand by it—whether the moment be favorable or not.' Have you ever experienced a successful day? With which for once a successful moment, a successful life, perhaps even a successful eternity might coincide?"

"Not yet. Obviously!"

"Obviously"?

"If I had experienced anything even remotely resembling that, I imagine, I should have to fear not only a nightmare for the following night but the cold sweats."

"Then your successful day is not even an idea, but only a dream?"

"Yes, except that instead of *having* it, I've *made* it in this essay. Look at my eraser, so black and small, look at the pile of pencil shavings below my window. Phrases and more phrases in the void, to no good purpose, addressed to a third incomprehensible something, though the two of us are not lost. Time and again in his epistles, not to the congregations, but to individuals, his helpers, Paul, from his prison in Rome, wrote about winter. For example, 'Do try to get here before winter. And when you come, bring the cloak I left with Carpus at Troas . . .' "

"And where is the cloak now? Forget the dream. See how the snow falls past the empty bird's nest. Arise to transubstantiation."

"To the next dream?"

PUBLISHER'S NOTE

Peter Handke and Ralph Manheim had a fruitful, long-standing collaboration and were accustomed to reviewing translations together. Mr. Manheim, who translated works by many internationally acclaimed writers, died shortly after completing his translation of two pieces included in this volume: *Essay on the Successful Day* and *Essay on Tiredness*. The final editing on these two essays was done after Mr. Manheim's death, with Mr. Handke's approval.